Marx Joyce
Abbott Hardy Machiavelli Chesterton Emerson Austen
Defoe Melville Montaigne Cooper Hugo Grimm
Carroll Haggard Eliot
Stoker Christie Molière
Wilde Maupassant Byron Schiller
Garnett Einstein Engels Smith Kafka
Goethe Fitzgerald Hawthorne Hall
Cotton Dostoyevsky Willis
Baum Kipling Doyle
Henry Nietzsche
Leslie Dumas Flaubert Turgenev Balzac
Stockton Vatsyayana Crane
Burroughs Verne
Curtis Tocqueville Gogol Vinci
Homer Widger Tolstoy Whitman Busch
Darwin Thoreau
Potter Freud Twain Scott
Kant Zola Lawrence Plato Harte
Jowett Stevenson Dickens
Andersen Burton Hesse
London Descartes Cervantes
Poe Aristotle Wells Voltaire Cooke
Hale James Hastings
Bunner Shakespeare Chambers Irving
Richter da
Doré Chekhov Benedict Alcott
Dante Shaw Pushkin
Swift Wodehouse Newton

Roman Britain in 1914

F. (Francis) Haverfield

Imprint

This book is part of TREDITION CLASSICS

Author: F. (Francis) Haverfield
Cover design: Buchgut, Berlin – Germany

Publisher: tredition GmbH, Hamburg - Germany
ISBN: 978-3-8472-2903-2

www.tredition.com
www.tredition.de

(A) Head of Silenus (1/1). Probably an artist's die,
for casting stamps for stamped ware (p. 20)

(B) Fragment of stamped ware (1/1), with ornament imitated from Samian (p. 19)

(C) Stamp for Mortarium (1/1)

Fig. 1. Pottery Stamps and Stamped Pottery from Holt.

[1]

TABLE OF CONTENTS

LIST OF ILLUSTRATIONS

23, 24. Margidunum, plan and seal-box. From the *Anti-quary*

25-28. Plan, section and views of the podium of the temple at Wroxeter. From the Report by Mr. Bushe-Fox

29. General plan of the Roman fort and precincts at Gellygaer. After plans by Mr. J. Ward

30. Postholes at Gellygaer

For the loan of blocks 14, 17-20, 21-2, and 23-4, I am indebted respectively to the Delegates of the Clarendon Press, Prof. Newstead, and the Liverpool University Press, the Morant Club and the Essex Archaeological Society, and the publisher of the *Antiquary*.

PREFACE

The contents of the present volume are of much the same character as those of its predecessor, 'Roman Britain in 1913'. The first section gives a retrospect of the chief finds made in 1914, so far as they are known to me. The second section is a more detailed and technical survey of the inscriptions found in Britain during that year. The third and longest section is a summary, with some attempt at estimate and criticism, of books and articles dealing with Roman Britain which appeared in 1914 or at least bear that date on cover or title-page. At the end I have added, for convenience, a list of the English archaeological and other publications which at least sometimes contain noteworthy articles relating to Roman Britain.

The total, both of finds and of publications, is smaller than in 1913. In part the outbreak of war in August called off various supervisors and not a few workmen from excavations then in progress; in one case it prevented a proposed excavation from being begun. It also seems to have retarded the issue of some archaeological periodicals. But the scarcity of finds is much more due to natural causes. The most extensive excavations of the year, those of Wroxeter and Corbridge, yielded little; they were both concerned with remains which had to be explored in the course of a complete uncovering of those sites but which were not in themselves very interesting. The lesser sites, too, were somewhat unproductive, though at least one, Traprain Law, is full of promise for the future, and good work has been done in the systematic examination of the fort at Ambleside and of certain rubbish-pits in London. In one case, that of Holt (pp. 15-21), where excavations have for the present come to an end, I have thought it well to include a brief retrospect of the whole of a very interesting series of finds and, aided by the kindness of the excavator, Mr. Arthur Acton of Wrexham, to add some illustrations of notable objects which have not yet appeared elsewhere in print.

A. RETROSPECT OF FINDS MADE IN 1914

i-xiv. Finds relating to the Roman Military Occupation.

(i) The exploration of the Roman-seeming earthworks in northern Scotland which Dr. Macdonald and I began in 1913 at Ythan Wells, in Aberdeenshire (Report for 1913, p. 7), was continued in 1914 by Dr. Macdonald at Raedykes, otherwise called Garrison Hill, three miles inland from Stonehaven. Here Roy saw and planned a large camp of very irregular outline, which he took to be Roman. 1 Since his time the ramparts have been somewhat ploughed down, but Dr. Macdonald could trace them round, identify the six gateways, and generally confirm Roy's plan, apart from its hill-shading. The ramparts proved to be of two kinds: part was built solidly of earth, with a deep ditch of Roman shape strengthened in places with clay, in front of it, while part was roughly piled with stones and defended only by a shallow rounded ditch. This difference seemed due to the differing nature of the ground; ditch and rampart were slighter where attack was less easy. The gateways were wide and provided with traverses (*tituli* or *tutuli*), as at Ythan Wells. No small finds were secured. The general character of the gateways and ramparts seemed to show Roman workmanship, but the exact date within the Roman period remained doubtful. It has been suggested that the traverses indicate Flavian rather than Antonine fortifying. But these devices are met with in Britain at Bar Hill, which presumably dates from about A.D. 140, and on Hadrian's Wall in third-century work.

(ii) *Wall of Pius and its forts.* At Balmuildy, north of Glasgow (see Report for 1913, p. 10), Mr. Miller has further cleared the baths outside the south-east corner of the fort and the adjacent ditches. The plan which I gave last year has now to be corrected so as to show a triple ditch between the south gate and the south-east corner and a double ditch from the south-east corner to the east gate. This latter [8] section of ditch was, however, filled up at some time with clay, and the bath planted on top of it. At presumably the same time a ditch was run out from the south-east corner so as to enclose the bath and form an annexe; in this annexe was found a broken altar-top with a few letters on it (below, p. 29). Search was also made for rubbish-pits on the north side of the fort, but without any result.

On other parts of the Wall Dr. Macdonald has gained further successes. Evidence seems to be coming out as to the hitherto missing forts of Kirkintilloch and Inveravon. More details have been secured of the fort at Mumrills—fully 4-1/2 acres in area and walled with earth, not with the turf or stone employed in the ramparts of the other forts of the Wall. The line of the Wall from Falkirk to Inveravon, a distance of four miles, has also been traced; it proved to be built of earth and clay, not of the turf used in the Wall westwards. Dr. Macdonald suggests that the eastern section of the Wall lay through heavily wooded country, where turf was naturally awanting.

(iii) *Traprain Law.* Very interesting, too, are the preliminary results secured by Mr. A. O. Curie on Traprain Law. This is an isolated hill in Haddingtonshire, some twenty miles east of Edinburgh, on the Whittingehame estate of Mr. Arthur Balfour. Legends cluster round it—of varying antiquity. It itself shows two distinct lines of fortification, one probably much older than the other, enclosing some 60 acres. The area excavated in 1914 was a tiny piece, about 30 yards square; the results were most promising. Five levels of stratification could be distinguished. The lowest and earliest yielded small objects of native work and Roman potsherds of the late first century: higher up, Roman coins and pottery of the second century appeared, and in the top level, Roman potsherds assigned to the fourth century. One Roman potsherd, from a second-century level, bore three Roman letters IRI, the meaning of which is likely to remain obscure. As the inscribed surface came from the inside of an urn, the writing must have been done after the pot was broken, and presumably on the hill itself. Among the native finds were stone and clay moulds for casting metal objects. The site, on a whole, seems to be native rather than Roman; it may be our first clue to the character of native *oppida* in northern Britain under Roman rule; its excavation is eminently worth pursuing.

(iv) *Northumberland, Hadrian's Wall.* On Hadrian's Wall no excavations have been carried out. But at Chesterholm two inscribed altars were found in the summer. One was dedicated to Juppiter Optimus Maximus; the rest of the lettering was illegible. The other, dedicated to Vulcan on behalf of the Divinity of the Imperial [9] House by the people of the locality, possesses much interest. The dedicators describe themselves as *vicani Vindolandenses*, and thus give proof that the civilians living outside the fort at Chesterholm formed a *vicus* or something that could plausibly be described as such; further, they teach the proper name of the place, which we have been wont to call Vindolana. See further below, p. 31.

North of the Wall, at Featherwood near High Rochester (the fort Bremenium) an altar has been found, dedicated to Victory (see p. 30).

(v) *Corbridge.* The exploration of Corbridge was carried through its ninth season by Mr. R. H. Forster. As in 1913, the results were somewhat scanty. The area examined, which lay on the north-east of the site, adjacent to the areas examined in 1910 and 1913, seems, like them, to have been thinly occupied in Roman times; at any rate the structures actually unearthed consisted only of a roughly built foundation (25 feet diam.) of uncertain use, which there is no reason to call a temple, some other even more indeterminate foundations, and two bits of road. More interest may attach to three ditches (one for sewage) and the clay base of a rampart, which belong in some way to the northern defences of the place in various times. The full meaning of these will, however, not be discernible till complete plans are available and probably not till further excavations have been made; Mr. Forster inclines to explain parts of them as ditches of a fort held in the age of Trajan, about A.D. 90-110. Several small finds merit note. An inscribed tile seems to have served as a writing lesson or rather, perhaps, as a reading lesson: see below, p. 32. The Samian pottery included a very few pieces of '29', a good deal of early '37', which most archaeologists would ascribe to the late first or the opening second century, and some other pieces which perhaps belong to a rather later part of the same century. The coins cover much the same period; few are later than Hadrian. Among them was a hoard of 32 denarii and 12 copper of which Mr. Craster has made the following list:—

Silver: 2 Republican, 1 Julius Caesar, 1 Mark Antony, 1 Nero, 1 Galba, 3 Vitellius, 13 Vespasian, 3 Titus, 6 Domitian, 1 unidentified.

Copper: 3 Vespasian, 1 Titus, 2 Domitian, 3 Nerva, 1 Trajan, 2 unidentified.

The latest coin was the copper of Trajan—a *dupondius* or Second Brass of A.D. 98. All the coins had been corroded into a single mass, apparently by the burning of a wooden box in which they have been kept; this burning must have occurred about A.D. 98-100. Among the bronze objects found during the year was a dragon-esque enamelled brooch.

(vi) In Upper *Weardale* (co. Durham) a peat-bog has given up two [10] bronze *paterae* or skillets, bearing the stamp of the Italian bronze-worker Cipius Polybius, and an uninscribed bronze ladle. See below, p. 33.

(vii) Near Appleby, at Hangingshaw farm, Mr. P. Ross has come upon a Roman inscription which proves to be a milestone of the Emperor Philip (A.D. 244-6) first found in 1694 and since lost sight of (p. 35).

(viii) *Ambleside Fort.* The excavation of the Roman fort in Borrans Field near Ambleside, noted in my Report for 1913 (p. 13), was continued by Mr. R. G. Collingwood, Fellow of Pembroke College, Oxford, and others with much success. The examination of the ramparts, gates, and turrets was completed; that of the main interior buildings was brought near completion, and a beginning was made on the barracks, sufficient to show that they were, at least in part, made of wood.

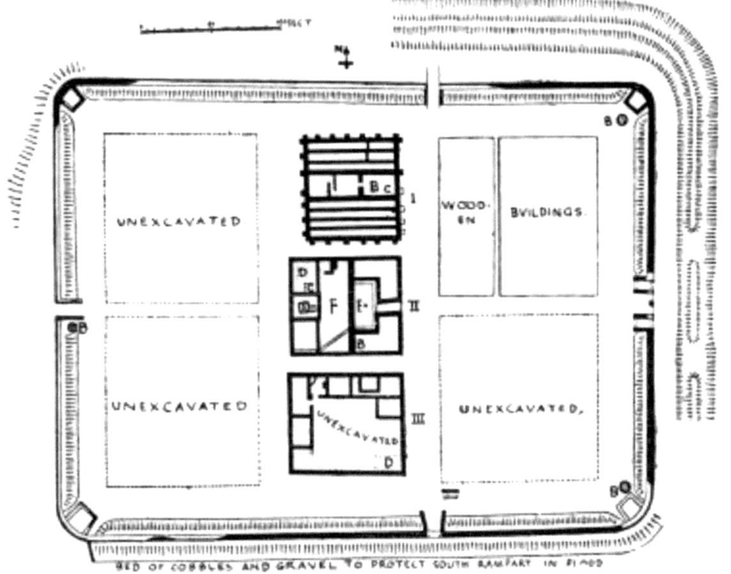

Fig. 2. Borrans Fort, Ambleside
(I. Granaries; II. Head-quarters; III. Commandant's House; A. Cellar;
B. Hearth or Kiln; C. Deposit of corn; D. Ditch perhaps belonging to
earliest fort; E. Outer Court of Head-quarters; F. Inner Court)

The fort, as is now clear (fig. 2), was an oblong enclosure of about
300 × 420 feet, nearly 3 acres. Round it ran a wall of roughly coursed
stone 4 feet thick, with a clay ramp behind and a ditch in front. Turrets stood at its corners. Four gates gave access to it; three of [11]
them were single and narrow, while the fourth, the east gate, was
double and was flanked by two guard-chambers. As usual, the chief
buildings stood in a row across the interior. Building I—see plan,
fig. 2—was a pair of granaries, each 66 feet long, with a space between. They were of normal plan, with external buttresses, base-
ment walls, and ventilating windows (not shown on plan). The
space between them, 15 feet wide, contained marks of an oven or
ovens (plan, B) and also some corn (plan, C) and may have been at
one time used for drying grain stored in the granaries; how far it
was roofed is doubtful. Building II, the Principia or Praetorium, a
structure of 68 × 76 feet, much resembled the Principia at Hardknot,

19

ten miles west of Ambleside, but possessed distinct features. As the plan shows, it had an entrance from the east, the two usual courts (EF), and the offices which usually face on to the inner court F. These offices, however, were only three in number instead of five, unless wooden partitions were used. Under the central office, the *sacellum* of the fort, where the standards and the altars for the official worship of the garrison are thought to have been kept, our fort had, at A, a sunk room or cellar, 6 feet square, entered by a stone stair. Such cellars occur at Chesters, Aesica, and elsewhere and probably served as strong-rooms for the regimental funds. At Chesters, the cellar had stone vaulting; at Ambleside there is no sign of this, and timber may have been used. In the northernmost room of the Principia some corn and woodwork as of a bin were noted (plan, C). The inner court F seemed to Mr. Collingwood to have been roofed; in its north end was a detached room, such as occurs at Chesters, of unknown use, which accords rather ill with a roof. In the colonnade round the outer court E were vestiges of a hearth or oven (plan, B). Building III (70 × 80 feet) is that usually called the commandant's house; it seems to show the normal plan of rooms arranged round a cloister enclosing a tiny open space. In buildings II and III, at D, traces were detected as of ditches and walling belonging to a fort older and probably smaller than that revealed by the excavation generally.

Small finds include coins of Faustina Iunior, Iulia Domna, and Valens, Samian of about A.D. 80 and later, including one or two bits of German Samian, a silver spoon, some glass, iron, and bronze objects, a leaden basin (?), and seven more leaden sling-bullets. It now seems clear that the fort was established about the time of Agricola (A.D. 80-5), though perhaps in smaller dimensions than those now visible, and was held till at least A.D. 365. Mr. Collingwood inclines to the view that it was abandoned after A.D. 85 and reoccupied under or about the time of Hadrian. The stratification of the turrets [12] seems to show that it was destroyed once or twice in the second or third centuries, but the evidence is not wholly clear in details. The granaries seem to have been rebuilt once and the rooms of the commandant's house mostly have two floors.

(ix) *Lancaster.* In October and November 1914, structural remains thought to be Roman, including 'an old Roman fireplace, circular in shape, with stone flues branching out', were noted in the garden of St. Mary's vicarage. The real meaning of the find seems doubtful.

(x) *Ribchester*. In the spring of 1913 a small school-building was pulled down at Ribchester, and the Manchester Classical Association was able to resume its examination of the Principia (praetorium) of the Roman fort, above a part of which this building had stood. The work was carried out by Prof. W. B. Anderson, of Manchester University, and Mr. D. Atkinson, Research Fellow of Reading College, and, though limited in extent, was very successful.

The first discovery of the Principia is due to Miss Greenall, who about 1905 was building a house close to the school and took care that certain remains found by her builders should be duly noted: excavations in 1906-7, however, left the size and extent of these remains somewhat uncertain and resulted in what we now know to be an incorrect plan. The work done last spring makes it plain (fig. 3) that the Principia fronted — in normal fashion — the main street of the fort (gravel laid on cobbles) running from the north to the south gate. But, abnormally, the frontage was formed by a verandah or colonnade: the only parallel which I can quote is from Caersws, where excavations in 1909 revealed a similar verandah in front of the Principia 2 . Next to the verandah stood the usual Outer Court with a colonnade round it and two wells in it (one is the usual provision): the colonnade seemed to have been twice rebuilt. Beyond that are fainter traces of the Inner Court which, however, lies mostly underneath a churchyard: the only fairly clear feature is a room (A on plan) which seems to have stood on the right side of the Inner Court, as at Chesters and Ambleside (fig. 2, above). Behind this, probably, stood the usual five office rooms. If we carry the Principia about 20 feet further back, which would be a full allowance for these rooms with their walling, the end of the whole structure will line with the ends of the granaries found some years ago. This, or something very like it, is what we should naturally expect. We then obtain a structure [13] measuring 81 × 112 feet, the latter dimension including a verandah 8 feet wide. This again seems a reasonable result. Ribchester was a large fort, about 6 acres, garrisoned by cavalry; in a similar fort at Chesters, on Hadrian's Wall, the Principia measured 85 × 125 feet: in the 'North Camp' at Camelon, another fort of much the same size (nearly 6 acres), they measured 92 × 120 feet.

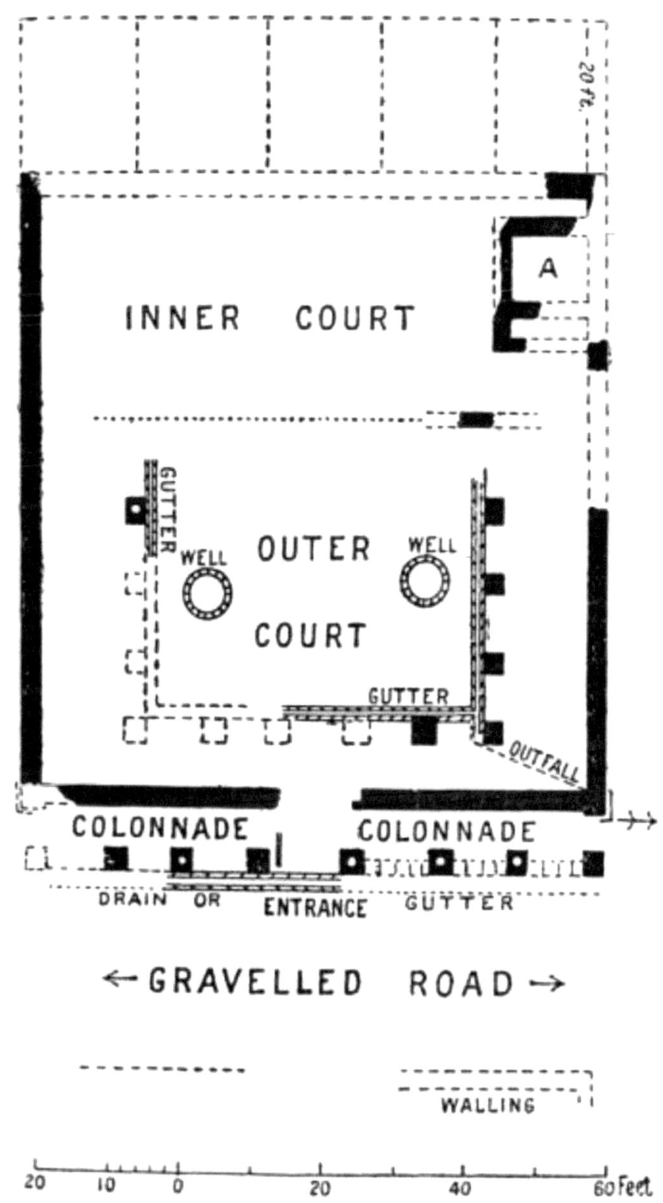

20 ft.
A
INNER COURT
GUTTER
WELL
OUTER
WELL
COURT
GUTTER
OUTFALL
COLONNADE
COLONNADE
DRAIN OR
ENTRANCE
GUTTER
GRAVELLED ROAD
WALLING
20 10 0 20 40 60 Feet

Fig. 3. Ribchester Fort, Head-quarters

(xi) *Slack.* The excavation of the Roman fort at Slack, near Huddersfield, noted in my report for 1913 (p. 14), was continued in 1914 by Mr. P. W. Dodd and Mr. A. M. Woodward, lecturers in Leeds University, which is doing good work in the exploration of southern Yorkshire. The defences of the fort, part of its central buildings (fig. 4, I-III), and part of its other buildings (B-K) have now been attacked. The defences consist of (1) a ditch 15 feet wide, possibly double on the north (more exactly north-west) side and certainly absent on the southern two-thirds of the east (north-east) [14] side; (2) a berme, 8 feet wide; and (3) a rampart 20-5 feet thick, built of turf and strengthened by a rough stone base which is, however, only 8-10 feet wide. Of the four gates, three (west, north, and east) have been examined; all are small and have wooden gate-posts instead of masonry. On each side of the east gate, which is the widest (15 ft.), the rampart is thought to thicken as if for greater defence. The absence of a ditch on the southern two-thirds of the east side may be connected with some paving outside the east gate and also with a bath-house, partly explored in 1824 and 1865, outside the south-east (east) corner; we may think that here was an annexe. The central buildings, so far as uncovered, are of stone; the Principia (III) perhaps had some wooden partitions. They are all ill-preserved and call for no further comment. West of them, in the rear of the fort, the excavators traced two long narrow wooden buildings (B, C), north of the road from the west (south-west) gate to the back of the Principia; on the other side of the road they found the ends of two similar buildings (D, E). This looks as if this portion of the fort was filled with four barracks. On the other side of the row of buildings I-III remains were traced of stone structures; one of these (F) had the L-shape characteristic of barracks, and indications point to two others (G, H) of the same shape. This implies six barrack buildings in this portion of the fort and ten barrack buildings in all, that is, a cohort 1,000 strong. But the [15] whole fort is only just 3 acres, and one would expect a smaller garrison; when excavations have advanced, we may perhaps find that the garrison was really a *cohors quingenaria* with six barracks, as at Gellygaer. Close against the east rampart, and indeed cutting somewhat into it, was a long thin building (K), 12-16 feet wide, which yielded much charcoal and potsherds and seemed an addition to the original plan of the fort.

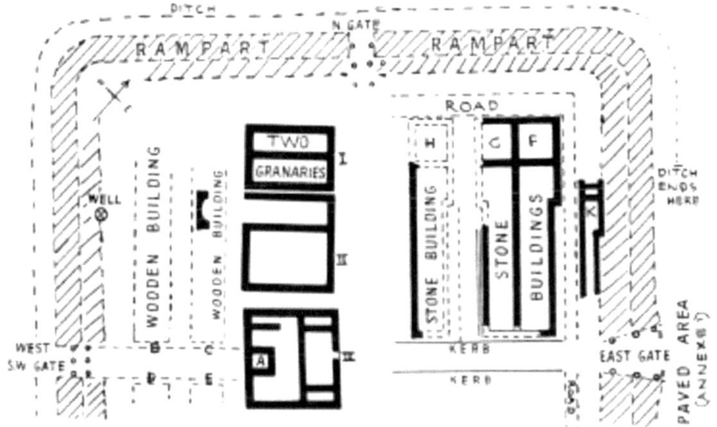

Fig. 4. Part of Slack Fort
(I. Granaries; II. Doubtful; III. Head-quarters; A. Shrine in III; B, C, D, E. Wooden buildings in western part of fort; F, G, H, K. Stone buildings in eastern part)

The few small finds included Samian of the late first and early second centuries (but no '29'), and a denarius of Trajan. In respect of date, they agree with the finds of last year and of 1865, and suggest that the fort was established under Domitian or Trajan, and abandoned under Hadrian or Pius; as an inscription of the Sixth Legion was found here in 1744, apparently in the baths, the evacuation cannot have been earlier than about A.D. 130. The occupation of Slack must therefore have resembled that of Castleshaw, which stands at the western end of the pass through the Pennine Hills, which Slack guards on the east. If this be so, an explanation must be discovered for two altars generally assigned to Slack. One of these, found three miles north of Slack at Greetland in 1597 among traces of buildings, is dated to A.D. 205 (CIL. vii. 200). The other, found two miles eastwards, at Longwood, in 1880 (Eph. Epigr. vii. 920), bears no date; but it was erected by an Aurelius Quintus to the Numina Augustorum, and neither item quite suits so early a date as the reign of Trajan. The dedication of the first is to the goddess Victoria — *Vic(toria) Brig(antia)* — that of the second *deo Berganti* (as well as the *Numina Aug.*); so that in each case a local shrine to a native deity may be concerned. It is also possible that a fort was built near Greetland, after the abandonment of Slack, to guard another pass over the Pennine, that by way of Blackstone Edge.

It is to be hoped that these interesting excavations may be continued and completed.

(xii) *Holt.* At Holt, eight miles south of Chester on the Denbighshire bank of the Dee, Mr. Arthur Acton has further explored the very interesting tile and pottery works of the Twentieth Legion, of which I spoke in my Report for 1913 (p. 15). The site is not even yet exhausted. But enough has been discovered to give a definite picture of it, and as it may perhaps not be possible to continue the excavations at present, and as the detailed report which Mr. Acton projects may take time to issue, I shall try here, with his permission, to summarize very briefly his most noteworthy results. I have to thank him for supplying me with much information and material for illustrations.

[16]

Holt combines the advantages of excellent clay for pottery and tile making, 3 good building stone (the Bunter red sandstone), and an easy waterway to Chester. Here the legion garrisoning Chester established, in the latter part of the first century, tile and pottery works for its own use and presumably also for the use of other neighbouring garrisons. Traces of these works were noted early in the seventeenth century, though they were not then properly understood. 4 In 1905 the late Mr. A. N. Palmer, of Wrexham, identified the site in two fields called Wall Lock and Hilly Field, just outside the village of Holt, and here, since 1906, Mr. Acton has, at his own cost, carefully and systematically carried out excavations.

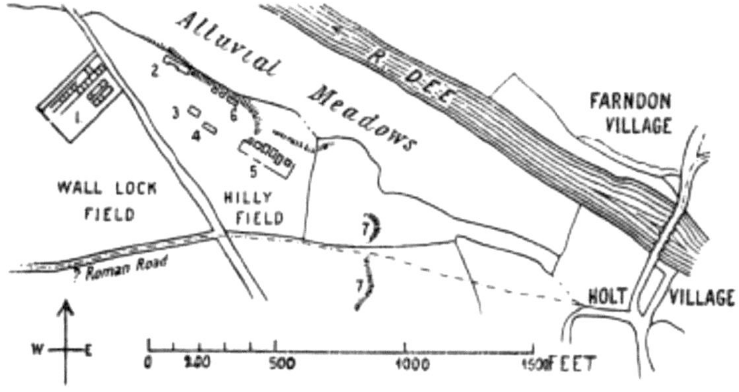

Fig. 5. Roman Site near Holt
(1. Barracks?; 2. Dwelling and Bath-house; 3. Kiln; 4. Drying-room,
&c. 5. Kilns; 6. Work-rooms?; 7. Clay-pits)

The discoveries show a group of structures scattered along a bank about a quarter of a mile in length which stands slightly above the Dee and the often flooded meadows beside it (fig. 5). At the west end of this area (fig. 5, no. 1, and fig. 6) was a large rectangular enclosure of about 62 × 123 yards (rather over 1-1/2 acres), girt with a strong wall 7 feet thick. Within it were five various rows of rooms mostly 15 feet square, with drains; some complicated masonry (? latrines) filled the east end. This enclosure was not wholly explored; it may have served for workmen's barracks; the contents of two rubbish-pits (fig. 6, aa) — bones of edible animals, cherry-stones, [17] shells of snails, and Dee mussels, potsherds, &c. — had a domestic look; mill-stones for grinding corn, including one bearing what seems to be a centurial mark, and fragments of buff imported amphorae were also found here. Between this enclosure and the river were two small buildings close together (fig. 5, no. 2 and fig. 7). The easternmost of these seems to have been a dwelling-house 92 feet long, with a corridor and two hypocausts; it may have housed the officer in charge of the potteries. The western building was a bath-house, with hot-rooms at the east end, and the dressing-room, latrine, and cold-bath at the west end; one side of this building was hewn into the solid rock to a height of 3 feet. Several fibulae were found in the drains of the bath-house.

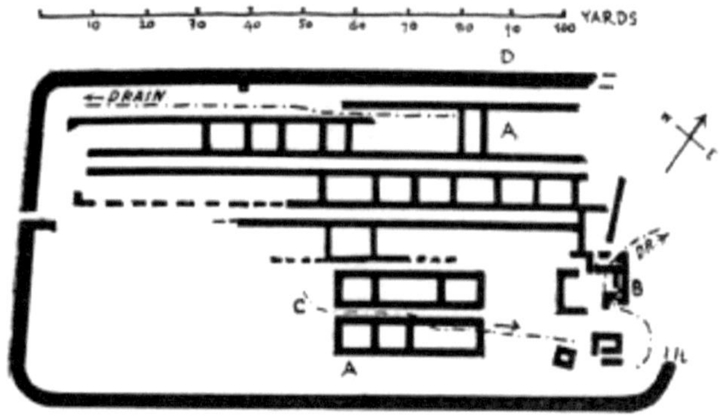

Fig. 6. Barracks (?), Holt
(A. Rubbish pits; B. Latrines?; C. Water-pipe; D. Bronze Age burial)

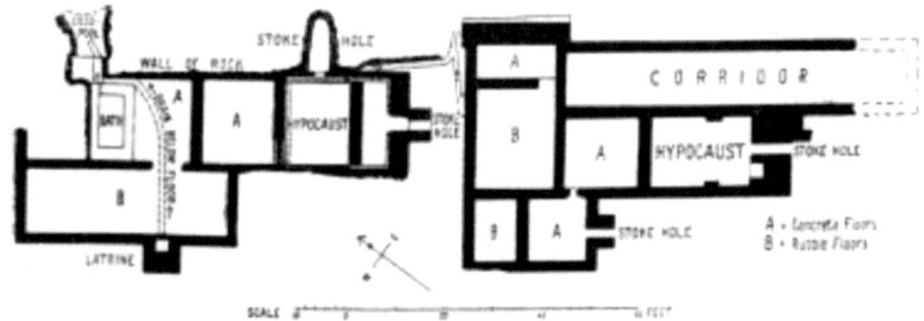

Fig. 7. Dwelling-house and Bath-house, Holt

The other structures (3, 4, 6, 7) served industrial purposes. No. 4 (fig. 5) contained a hypocaust and was perhaps a workroom and drying shed. At 6 were ill-built and ill-preserved rooms, containing [18] puddled clay, potsherds, &c., which declared them to be work-sheds of some sort. Finally, at 3 and 5 we have the kilns. No. 3 was a kiln 17 feet square, with a double flue, used (as its contents showed) for potting, and indeed for fine potting. No. 5 (figs. 8, 9) was an elaborate 'plant' of eight kilns in an enclosure of about 55 × 140 feet. Kilns A, B, F, H were used for pottery, C, D, E for tiles, F for both large vessels and tiles; the circular kiln G seems to be a later addi-tion to the original plan. The kilns were thus grouped together for economy in handling the raw and fired material and in stacking the fuel, and also for economy of heat; the three tile-kilns in the centre would be charged, fired, and drawn in turn, and the heat from them would keep warm the smaller pottery-kilns round them. The interiors of the kilns contained many broken and a few perfect pots and tiles; round them lay an enormous mass of wood-ashes, broken tiles and pots, 'wasters' and the like. The wood-ashes seem to be mainly oak, which abounds in the neighbourhood of Holt. The kilns themselves are exceptionally well-preserved. They must have been in actual working order, when abandoned, and so they illustrate — perhaps better than any kilns as yet uncovered and recorded in any Roman province — the actual mechanism of a Roman tile- or pottery-kiln. The construction of a kiln floor, which shall work effectively and accurately, is less simple than it looks; the adjustment of the heat to the class of wares to be fired, the distribution of the heat by [19] proper flues and by vent-holes of the right size, and other such details require knowledge and care. The remains at Holt show these features admirably, and Mr. Acton has been able to examine them with the aid of two of our best experts on pottery-making, Mr. Wm. and Mr. Joseph Burton, of Manchester.

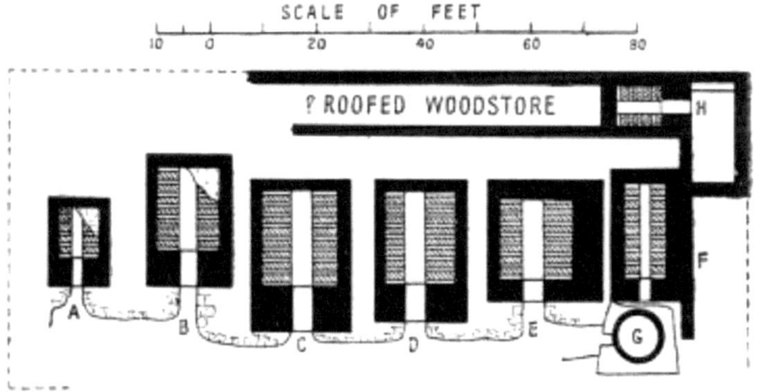

Fig. 8. Plan of Kiln-plant at Holt (see p. 34, and Fig. 9)
(Except at kilns F, G, the letters on the plan are placed at the fire-holes. In kilns A, B a small piece of the kiln floor (on which the vessels were placed for baking) is shown diagrammatically, to illustrate

the relation between the hot-air holes in the floors and the passages
in the underlying heating-chambers)

Fig. 9. Restoration of the Holt Kiln-plant, showing the floors on
which the Tiles or Vessels were piled for Baking (p. 18)
The letters ABCDE are placed at the mouths of the stoke-holes of
the respective kilns. Kilns ABDFH were used for pottery, CDE for
tiles, F for large vessels and for tiles; G seems an addition to the
original plan.

Smaller finds include two centurial stones (one found in 1914 is
described below, p. 34); a mill-stone with letters suggesting that it
belonged to a century of soldiers; several *graffiti*, mostly of a military character, so far as one can decipher them (for one see my Report for 1913, p. 30); a profusion of stamped tiles of the Twentieth
Legion, mostly 'wasters'; some two dozen antefixes of the same
legion; several tile and pottery stamps; about 45 coins of various
dates; much window glass, and an immense quantity of potsherds
of the most various kinds. Among these latter were Samian pieces
of the late first century (no '29', but early '37' and '78' and a stamp of
CRESTO) and of the second century (including the German stamp
IANVF), and imitation Samian made on the spot. A quantity of lead
and of iron perhaps worked into nails, &c., at Holt, and a few cruci-
bles for casting small bronze objects, may also be mentioned.

The Twentieth Legion tiles at Holt bear stamps identical with those on its tiles at Chester; we may think that the legion made for itself at Holt most of the tiles which it used in its fortress. Equal interest and more novelty attaches to the pottery made at Holt. This comprises many varieties; most prominent is a reddish or buff ware of excellent character, coated with a fine slip, which occurs in many different forms of vessels, cooking pots, jars, saucers, and even large flat dishes up to 30 inches in diameter. Specimens of these occur also in Chester, and it is clear that the legionary workmen made not only tiles — as in legionary tile-works in other lands — but also pots, mortaria (fig. 1), &c., for legionary use.

Perhaps the most remarkable pieces among the pottery are some stamped pieces copied from decorated Samian, which I am able to figure here by Mr. Acton's kindness (figs. 1, 10, 11). They are pale reddish-brown in colour and nearly as firm in texture as good Samian; they are made (he tells me) by throwing on a wheel a clay (or 'body') prepared from local materials, then impressing the stamps, and finally laying on an iron oxide slip, perhaps with a brush. Sir Arthur Evans has pointed out to me that the stamp used for the heads on fig. 1 was a gem set in a ring; the setting is clearly visible under each head. The shape and ornament have plainly been suggested by specimens of Samian '37' bowls, probably of the second century. How far the author tried to copy definite pieces of Samian and how far he aimed at [20] giving the general effect, is not quite clear to me. The large circles on fig. 11 suggest the medallions of Lezoux potters like Cinnamus; the palmettes might have been taken from German originals. Very few of these interesting pieces were found — all of them close to the kiln numbered 3 on fig. 5.

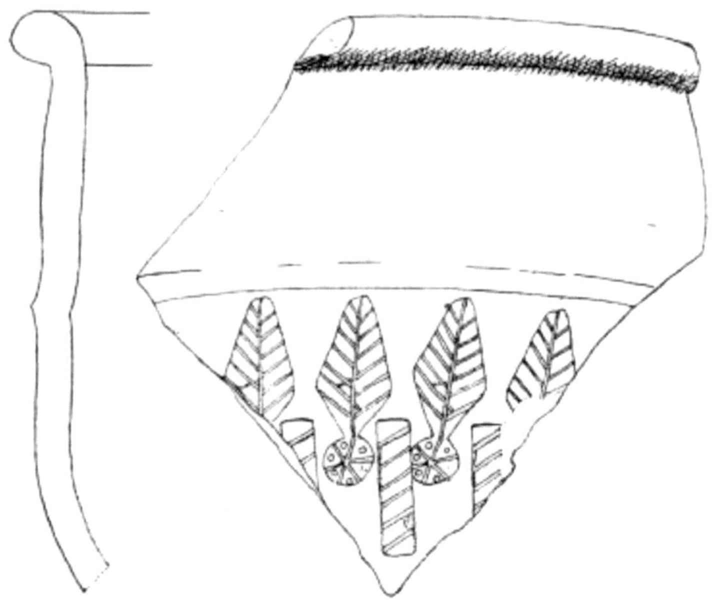

Fig. 10. Holt, Stamped Ware in imitation of Samian, Shape 37 (1/1)

An even more striking piece (fig. 1) is a 'poinçon' bearing the head of Silenus in relief. It is believed to be the artist's die, from which the potters' sunk dies would be cast; from such sunk dies little casts would be made and 'applied' in relief to the outsides of the bowls, to the handles of jugs, &c. It does not seem to have been intended for any sort of ware made from a mould; indeed, moulded ware rarely occurs among the products of Holt. It is far finer work than most Samian ornamentation; probably, however, it has never been damaged by use. It was found, with one or two less remarkable dies, in the waste round kiln 3.

Interest attaches also to various vessels, two or three nearly perfect and many broken, which have been glazed with green, brown or yellow glaze; some of these pieces seem to be imitated from cut glass ware. Along with them Mr. Acton has found the containing bowls (saggars) [21] and kiln-props used to protect and support the glazed vessels during the process of firing, and as the drip of the glaze is visible on the sides of the props and the bottoms of the saggars, he infers that the Holt potters manufactured glazed ware with success.

Fig. 11. Stamped Ware, in Imitation of Samian, Shape 37 (1/1). (See pp. 19, 20)

It is obvious that Mr. Acton's detailed report on Holt will be full of important matter, and that further excavation of the site, whenever it may be possible, will also yield important results.

(xiii) *Cardiff.* The widening of Duke Street, which fronts the eastern half of the south side of Cardiff Castle, has revealed the southeast angle of the Roman fort, on the top of which the castle stands, and has revealed it in good preservation. Nothing, however, has come to light which seems to increase or alter our previous knowledge of the fort. Many small Roman objects are stated to have been found, Samian ware, coins, brooches, beads, in the course of the work; these may belong to the 'civil settlement' which, as I have said elsewhere, may have lain to the south of the fort (*Military Aspects of Roman Wales*, p. 105). When they have been sorted and dated, they should throw light on the history of Roman Cardiff.

(xiv) *Richborough.* This important site has been taken over by H.M. Office of Works, and some digging has been done round the central platform, but (Mr. Peers tells me) without any notable result. The theory that this platform was the base of a lighthouse is still the most probable.

xv-xxv. Finds relating to Civil Life

(xv) *Wroxeter (Viroconium)*. The systematic excavation of Wroxeter begun in 1912 by Mr. J. P. Bushe-Fox on behalf of the London Society of Antiquaries and the Shropshire Archaeological Society, was carried by him through its third season in 1914. The area examined lay immediately north of the temple uncovered in 1913. The main structure in it was a large dwelling-house 115 feet long, with extensions up to 200 feet, which possessed at least two courtyards, a small detached bath-house, various mosaic and cement floors, hypocausts, and so forth. It had been often altered, and its excavation and explanation were excessively difficult. Mr. Bushe-Fox thinks that it may have begun as three shops giving on to the north and south Street which bounds its eastern end. Certainly it became, in course of time, a large corridor-house with a south aspect and an eastern wing fronting the street, and as such it underwent several changes in detail. Beyond its western end lay a still more puzzling structure. An enceinte formed by two parallel walls, about 13 feet apart, enclosed a rectangular space of about 150 feet wide; the western end [22] of it, and therefore its length, could not be ascertained; the two corners uncovered at the east end were rounded; an entrance seems to have passed through the north-east corner. It has been called a small fort, an amphitheatre, a stadium, and several other things. But a fort should be larger and would indeed be somewhat hard to account for at this spot; while a stadium should have a rounded end and, if it was of orthodox length, would have extended outside the town into or almost into the Severn. Interest attaches to a water-channel along the main (north and south) street. This was found to have at intervals slits in each side which were plainly meant for sluice-gates to be let down; Mr. Bushe-Fox thinks that the channel was a water-supply, and not an outfall, and that by the sluice-gates the water was dammed up so as, when needed, to flow along certain smaller channels into the private houses which stood beside the road. If so, the discovery has much interest; the arrangement is peculiar, but no other explanation seems forthcoming.

Small finds were many and good. Mr. Bushe-Fox gathered 571 coins ranging from three British and one or two Roman Republican issues, to three early coins of the Emperor Arcadius, over 200 Samian potters' stamps, and much Samian datable to the period about A.D. 75-130, with a few rare pieces of the pre-Flavian age. There was a noticeable scarcity of both Samian and coins of the post-Hadrianic, Antonine period; it was also observed that recognizable 'stratified deposits' did not occur after the age of Hadrian. Among individual objects attention is due to a small seal-box, with wax for the seal actually remaining in it.

It appears that it will probably not be possible to continue this excavation, even on a limited scale, next summer. Mr. Bushe-Fox's report for 1913 is noticed below, p. 52.

(xvi) *Lincoln.* At Lincoln an inscribed fragment found in 1906 has now come to light. It bears only three letters, IND, being the last letters of the inscription; these plainly preserve a part of the name of the town, Lindum. See below, p. 34.

(xvii) *Gloucester.* Here, in March 1914, a mosaic floor, 16 feet square, with a complex geometrical pattern in red, white, and blue, has been found 9 feet below the present surface, at 22 Northgate Street. Some painted wall-plaster from the walls of the room to which it belonged were found with it.

(xviii) Discoveries in *London* have been limited to two groups of rubbish-pits in the City, (*a*) At the General Post Office the pits opened in 1913 (see my Report, p. 22) were further carefully explored in 1914 by Mr. F. Lambert, Mr. Thos. Wilson, and Dr. Norman; [23] the Post Office gave full facilities. Over 100 'potholes' were detected, of which about forty yielded more or less datable rubbish, mainly potsherds. Four contained objects of about A.D. 50-80, though not in great quantity—four bits of decorated Samian and eight Samian stamps—and fourteen contained objects of about A.D. 70-100; the rest seemed to belong to the second century, with some few later items intermixed. One would infer that a little rubbish was deposited here before the Flavian period, but that after about A.D. 70 or 80 the site was freely used as a rubbish-ground for three generations or more. Two objects may be noted, a gold ring bearing the owner's initials Q.D.D. and a bit of inscribed wood from the lining of a well or pit (p. 35). (*b*) At the top of King William Street, between Sherborne Lane and Abchurch Lane, not so far from the Mansion

House, five large pits were opened in the summer of 1914, in the course of ordinary contractors' building work. They could not be so minutely examined as the Post Office pits, but it was possible to observe that their datable potsherds fell roughly within the period A.D. 50-100, and that a good many potsherds were earlier than the Flavian age; there must have been considerable deposit of rubbish here before A.D. 70 or thereabouts, and it must have ceased about the end of the century. A full account of both groups of pits was given to the Society of Antiquaries by Mr. F. Lambert on February 11, 1915; illustrated notices of the Post Office finds were contributed by Mr. Thos. Wilson to the Post Office Magazine, *St. Martin-le-Grand* (January and July, 1914); Mr. D. Atkinson helped with the dating of the pottery.

Much gratitude is due to those who have so skilfully collaborated to achieve these results. So far as it is permissible to argue from two sites only, they seem to throw real light on the growth of the earliest Roman London. The Post Office pits lie in the extreme north-west of the later Londinium, just inside the walls; the King William Street pits are in its eastern half, not far from the east bank of the now vanished stream of Wallbrook, which roughly bisected the whole later extent of the town. It may be assumed that, at the time when the two groups of pits were in use, the inhabited area had not yet spread over their sites, though it had come more or less close. That would imply that the earliest city lay mainly, though perhaps not wholly, on the east bank of Wallbrook; then, as the houses spread and the town west of Wallbrook developed, the King William Street pits were closed, while the Post Office pits came more into use, during and after the Flavian age.

This conclusion is tentative. It must be remembered that the [24] stratification of rubbish-pits, ancient as well as modern, is often very peculiar. It is liable to be confused by all sorts of cross-currents. In particular, objects are constantly thrown into rubbish-pits many years, perhaps even centuries, after those objects have passed out of use. Whenever, even in a village, an old cottage is pulled down or a new one built, old rubbish gets shifted to new places and mixed with rubbish of a quite different age. At Caerwent, as Dr. T. Ashby once told me, a deep rubbish-pit yielded a coin of about A.D. 85 at a third of the way down, and at the very bottom a coin of about 315.

That is, the pit was in use about or after 315; some one then shovelled into it debris of much earlier date. The London pits now in question are, however, fairly uniform in their contents, and their evidence may be utilized at least as a base for further inquiries.

(xix-xxii) *Rural dwellings*. Three Roman 'villas'—that is, country-houses or farms—have been explored in 1914. All are small.

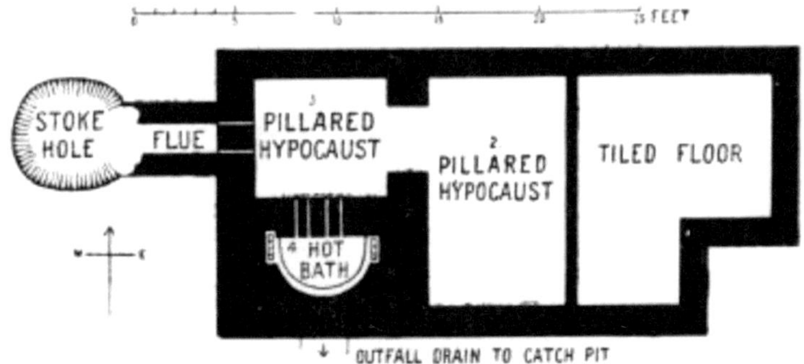

Fig. 12. Bath-house, East Grimstead

(xix) At *East Grimstead*, five miles south-east from Salisbury, on Maypole Farm near Churchway Copse 5 , a bath-house has been dug out and planned by Mr. Heywood Sumner, to whom I owe the following details. The building (fig. 12) measures only 14 × 28 feet and contains only four rooms, (1) a tile-paved apartment which probably served as entrance and dressing-room, (2) a room over a pillared hypocaust, which may be called the tepidarium, (3) a similar smaller room, nearer the furnace and therefore perhaps hotter, which may be the caldarium—though really it is hardly worth while to distinguish between these two rooms—and (4) a semicircular bath, lined with pink mortar and fine cement, warmed with flues from rooms 3 and with box-tiles, and provided with an outfall drain; east of rooms 3 and 4 was the furnace. Small finds included window glass, potsherds, two to three hundred oyster-shells, and five Third Brass coins (two Constantinian, three illegible). Large stone foundations [25] have been detected close by; presumably this was the detached bath-house for a substantial residence which awaits excavation. Such detached bath-houses are common; I may instance one found in 1845 at Wheatley (Oxon.), which had very similar internal arrangements and stood near a substantial dwelling-house not yet explored (*Archaeol. Journal*, ii. 350). A full description of the Grimstead bath, by Mr. Sumner, is in the press.

(xx) Three miles south-west of Guildford, at Limnerslease in the parish of *Compton*, Mr. Mill Stephenson has helped to uncover a house measuring 53 × 76 feet, with front and back corridors, and seven rooms, including baths. Coins suggested that it was inhabited in the early fourth century—a period when our evidence shows that many Romano-British farms and country-houses were occupied. 6

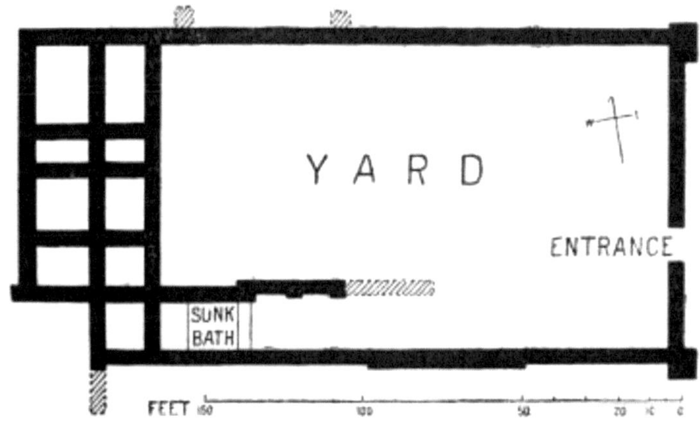

Fig. 13. House at North Ash, Kent

(xxi) A third house is supplied by Kent. This was found in June about six miles south of Gravesend, near the track from *North Ash* to Ash Church, on the farm of Mr. Geo. Day. Woodland was being cleared for an orchard, flint foundations were encountered, and the site was then explored by Mr. Jas. Kirk, Mr. S. Priest, and others of the Dartford Antiquarian Society, to whom I am indebted for information: the Society will in due course issue a full Report. The spade (fig. 13) revealed a rectangular walled enclosure of 53 × 104 feet. The entrance was at the east end; the dwelling-rooms (including a sunk bath, 7 feet square, lined with plaster) were, so far as traced, in the west and south-west portion; much of the walled space may have been farmyard or wooden sheds. Many bits of Samian and other pottery were found (among them a mortarium stamped MARTINVSF), and many oyster-shells. Other Romano-British foundations have been suspected close by.

[26]

The structure somewhat resembles the type of farm-house which might fairly be called, from its best-known example — the only one now uncovered to view — the Carisbrooke type. 7 That, however, usually has rooms at both ends, as in the Clanville example which I figure here as more perfect than the Carisbrooke one (fig. 14). One might compare the buildings at Castlefield, Finkley, and Holbury, which I have discussed in the *Victoria History of Hants* (i. 302-3, 312), and which were perhaps rudimentary forms of the Carisbrooke type.

CLANVILLE

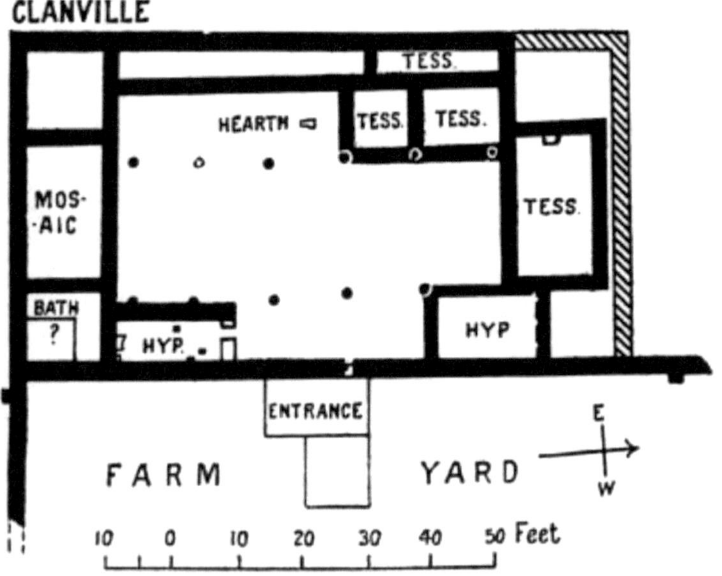

Fig. 14. Farm-house at Clanville, Kent (To illustrate Fig. 13)

(xxii) A few kindred items may be grouped here. Digging has been attempted in a Roman 'villa' at Litlington (Cambs.) but, as Prof. McKenny Hughes tells me, with little success. The 'beautifully tiled and marbled floors' are newspaper exaggeration. A 'Roman bath' which was stated to have been found early in 1914 at Kingston-on-Thames, in the work of widening the bridge, is declared by Mr. Mill Stephenson not to be Roman at all. Lastly, an excavation of an undoubted Roman house at Broom Farm, between Hambledon and Soberton in south-east Hants, projected by Mr. A. Moray Williams, was prevented by the war, which called Mr. Williams to serve his country.

[27]

(xxiii) *Lowbury.* During the early summer of 1914 Mr. D. Atkinson completed his examination of the interesting site of Lowbury, high amid the east Berkshire Downs. Of the results which he won in 1913 I gave some account last year (Report for 1913, p. 22); those of 1914 confirm and develop them. We may, then, accept the site as, at first and during the Middle Empire, a summer farm or herdsmen's shelter, and in the latest Roman days a refuge from invading English. Whether the wall which he traced round the little place was reared to keep in cattle or to keep out foes, is not clear; possibly enough, it served both uses. In all, Mr. Atkinson gathered about 850 coins belonging to all periods of the Empire but especially to the latest fourth century and including Theodosius, Arcadius, and Honorius. He also found over fifty brooches and a great amount of pottery — 3 cwt., he tells me — which was mostly rough ware: there was little Samian (some of shape '37'), less Castor, and hardly any traces of mortaria. A notable find was the skeleton of a woman of 50 (ht. about 5 feet 9 inches), which he discovered in the trench dug to receive the foundations of the enclosing wall; it lay in the line of the foundations amidst the perished cement of the wall, and its associations and position forbid us to think either that it was buried before the wall was thought of or was inserted after the wall was ruined. Mr. Atkinson formed the theory — with natural hesitation — that it might be a foundation burial, and I understand that Sir Jas. Frazer accepts this suggestion. A full report of the whole work will shortly be issued in the Reading College Research Series.

(xxiv) *Eastbourne, Beachy Head.* The Rev. W. Budgen, of Eastbourne, tells me of a hoard of 540 coins found in 1914 in a coombe near Bullock Down, just behind Beachy Head. The coins range from

Valerian (1 coin) to Quintillus (4 coins) and Probus (1 coin); 69 are attributed to Gallienus, 88 to Victorinus, 197 to the Tetrici, and 40 to Claudius Gothicus ; the hoard may have been buried about A.D. 280, but it has to be added that 130 coins have not been yet identified. Hoards of somewhat this date are exceedingly common; in 1901 I published accounts of two such hoards detected, shortly before that, at points quite close to the findspot of the present hoard (see *Sussex Archaeological Collections*, xliv, pp. 1-8).

Mr. Budgen has also sent me photographs of some early cinerary urns and a 'Gaulish' fibula, found together in Eastbourne in 1914. The things may belong to the middle of the first century A.D. The 'Gaulish' type of fibula has been discussed and figured by Sir Arthur Evans (*Archaeologia*, lv. 188-9, fig. 10; see also Dressel's note in [28] *Bonner Jahrbücher*, lxiv. 82). Its home appears to be Gaul. In Britain it occurs rather infrequently; east of the Rhine it is still rarer; it shows only one vestige of itself at Haltern and is wholly absent from Hofheim and the Saalburg. Its date appears to be the first century A.D., and perhaps rather the earlier two-thirds than the end of that period.

(xxv) *Parc-y-Meirch* (*North Wales*). Here Mr. Willoughby Gardner has further continued his valuable excavations (Report for 1913, p. 25). The new coin-finds seem to hint that the later fourth-century stratum may have been occupied earlier in that century than the date which I gave last year, A.D. 340. But the siege of this hill-fort is bound to be long and its full results will not be clear till the end. Then we may expect it to throw real light on an obscure corner of the history of Roman and also post-Roman Wales.

[29]

B. ROMAN INSCRIPTIONS FOUND IN BRITAIN IN 1914

This section includes the Roman inscriptions which have been found, or (perhaps I should say) first recognized to exist, in Britain in 1914 or which have become more accurately known in that year. As in 1913, the list is short and its items are not of great importance; but the Chesterholm altar (No. 5) deserves note, and the Corbridge tile also possesses considerable interest.

I have edited them in the usual manner, first stating the origin, character, &c., of the inscription, then giving its text with a rendering in English, thirdly adding any needful notes and acknowledging obligations to those who may have communicated the items to me. In the expansions of the text, square brackets denote letters which, owing to breakage or other cause, are not now on the stone, though one may presume that they were originally there; round brackets denote expansions of Roman abbreviations. The inscriptions are printed in the same order as the finds in section A, that is, from north to south—though with so few items the order hardly matters.

(1) Found at Balmuildy (above, p. 7) in the annexe to the south-east of the fort proper, some sandstone fragments from the top of a small altar, originally perhaps about 14 inches wide. At the top, in a semicircular panel is a rude head; below are letters from the first two lines of the dedication; probably the first line had originally four letters:—

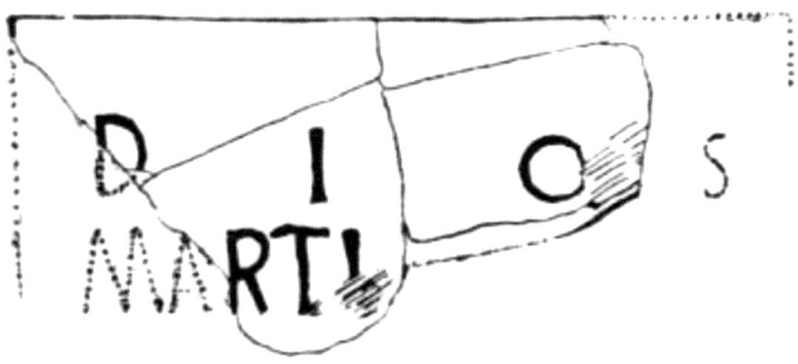

Fig. 15

Possibly DIO may be for *deo*. It is by no means a common orthography, but if it be accepted, we can read *dio [s(ancto) Ma]rti....* The reading DIIO, *deo*, is I fear impossible.

I have to thank Mr. S. N. Miller, the excavator, for photographs.

[30]

(2) At Traprain Law (above, p. 8) a small potsherd from a second-century level bore the letters scratched on it

IRI⁄

These letters were on the side of the potsherd which had formed the inner surface when the pot was whole; they must therefore have been inscribed after the pot had been smashed, and the size and shape of the bit give cause to think that it may have been broken intentionally for inscription—possibly for use in some game. In any case, it must have been inscribed at Traprain Law, and not brought there already written, and the occurrence of writing of any sort on such a site is noteworthy.

I am indebted to Dr. G. Macdonald for a sight of the piece.

(3) Found about three and a half miles north of the Roman fort Bremenium, High Rochester, near Horsley in north Northumberland, beside the Roman road over the Cheviots (Dere Street), close to the steading of Featherwood, in the autumn of 1914, now in the porch of Horsley Parish Church, a plain altar 51 inches high by 22 inches wide, with six lines of letters 2 inches tall. The inscription is unusually illegible. Only the first and last lines are readable with certainty; elsewhere some letters can be read or guessed, but not so as to yield coherent sense.

VICTORIAE	(only bottom of final E visible)
ET IVL	(ET probable, IVL fairly certain)
MEIANIC	(only M quite certain)
II C	(erased on purpose)

PVBLICO
V · S · L *m*

The altar was dedicated to Victory; nothing else is certain. It is tempting to conjecture in line 2 ET N AVG, *et numinibus Augustorum*, as on some other altars to Victory, but ET is not certain, though probable, and N AVG is definitely improbable. The fourth line seems to have been intentionally erased. I find no sign of any mention of the Cohors I Vardullorum, which garrisoned Bremenium, though it or its commander might naturally be concerned in putting up such an altar.

We may assume that the altar belongs to Bremenium; possibly it was brought thence when Featherwood was built.

I have to thank the Rev. Thos. Stephens, vicar of Horsley, for photographs and an excellent squeeze and readings, and Mr. R. Blair for a photograph.

[31]

(4-5) Found on July 17, 1914, at Chesterholm, just south of Hadrian's Wall, lying immediately underneath the surface in a grass field 120 yards west of the fort, two altars:

(4) 32 inches tall, 15 inches broad, illegible save for the first line

IOM

I(ovi) o(ptimo) m(aximo)....

(5) 34 inches tall, 22 inches broad, with 8 lines of rather irregular letters, not quite legible at the end (fig. 16).

Fig. 16. Altar from Chesterholm

Pro domu divina et numinibus Augustorum, Volcano sacrum, vicani Vindolandesses, cu[r(am)] agente ... v(otum) s(olvit) l(ibens) m(erito).

'For the Divine (i.e. Imperial) House and the Divinity of the Emperors, dedicated to Vulcan by the members of the *vicus* of Vindolanda, under the care of ... (name illegible).'

The statement of the reason for the dedication given in the first three lines is strictly tautologous, the Divine House and the Divinity [32] of the Emperors being practically the same thing. The formula *numinibus Aug.* is very common in Britain, though somewhat rare elsewhere; in other provinces its place is supplied by the formula *in honorem domus divinae*; it belongs mostly to the late second and third centuries. The plural *Augustorum* does not appear to refer to a plurality of reigning Emperors, but to the whole body of Emperors dead and living who were worshipped in the Cult of the Emperors.

The *vicani Vindolandesses* are the members of the settlement—women and children, traders, old soldiers, and others—which grew up outside the fort at Chesterholm, as outside nearly all Roman forts and fortresses. In this case they formed a small self-governing community, presumably with its own 'parish council', which could be called by the Roman term *vicus*, even if it was not all that a proper *vicus* should be. This altar was put up at the vote of their 'parish meeting' and paid for, one imagines, out of their common funds. The term *vicus* is applied to similar settlements outside forts on the German Limes; thus we have the *vicani Murrenses* at the fort of Benningen on the Murr (CIL. xiii. 6454) and the *vicus Aurelius* or *Aurelianus* at Oehringen (ibid. 6541).

Vindolandesses, which is merely a phonetic spelling or misspelling of *Vindolandenses*, gives the correct name of the fort. In the Notitia it is spelt Vindolana, in the Ravennas (431. 11) Vindolanda; and as in general the Ravennas teems with errors and the Notitia is fairly correct, the spelling Vindolana has always been preferred, although (as Prof. Sir John Rhys tells me) its second part *-lana* is an etymological puzzle. It now appears that in this, as in some few other cases, the Ravennas has kept the true tradition. The termination *-landa* is a Celtic word denoting a small defined space, akin to the Welsh 'llan', and also to the English 'land'; I cannot, however, find any other example in which it forms part of a place-name of Roman date. *Vindo-* is connected either with the adjective *vindos*, 'white', or with the personal name Vindos derived from that adjective.

I have to thank Mrs. Clayton, the owner of Chesterholm, and her foreman, Mr. T. Hepple, for excellent photographs and squeezes. The altars are now in the Chesters Museum.

(6) Found at Corbridge, in August 1914, fragment of a tile, 7 × 8 inches in size, on which, before it was baked hard, some one had scratched three lines of lettering about 1-1-1/2 inches tall; the sur-

viving letters form the beginnings of the lines of which the ends are broken off. There were never more than three lines, apparently.

[33]

O M Q ∟

L �II N D/

L E G E F E L

The inscription seems to have been a reading lesson. First the teacher scratched two lines of letters, in no particular order and making no particular sense; then he added the exhortation *lege feliciter*, 'read and good luck to you'. A modern teacher, even though he taught by the aid of a slate in lieu of a soft tile, might have expressed himself less gracefully. The tile may be compared with the well-known tile from Silchester, on which Maunde Thompson detected a writing lesson (Eph. Epigr. ix. 1293). A knowledge of reading and writing does not seem to have been at all uncommon in Roman Britain or in the Roman world generally, even among the working classes; I may refer to my *Romanization of Roman Britain* (ed. 3, pp. 29-34).

The imperfectly preserved letter after Q in line 1 was perhaps an angular L or E; that after D, in line 2, may have been M or N or even A.

I am indebted to Mr. R. H. Forster for a photograph and squeeze of the tile.

(7) Found in a peat-bog in Upper Weardale, in August 1913, two bronze skillets or 'paterae', of the usual saucepan shape, the larger weighing 15-1/2 oz., the smaller 8-1/2 oz. Each bore a stamp on the handle; the smaller had also a graffito on the rim of the bottom made by a succession of little dots. An uninscribed bronze ladle was found with the 'paterae':

(*a*) on the larger patera: **P CIPE POLI**

(*b*) on the smaller: **pOLYBI · I**

(*c*) punctate: **LICINIANI**

The stamps of the Campanian bronze-worker Cipius Polybius are well known. Upwards of forty have been found, rather curiously distributed (in the main) between Pompeii and places on or near the Rhenish and Danubian frontiers, in northern Britain, and in German and Danish lands outside the Roman Empire. The stamped 'paterae' of other Cipii and other bronze-workers have a somewhat similar distribution; it seems that the objects were made in the first century A.D., in or near Pompeii, and were chiefly exported to or beyond the borders of the Empire. Their exact use is still uncertain, I have discussed them in the *Archaeological Journal*, xlix, 1892, pp. 228-31; they have since been treated more fully by H. Willers (*Bronzeeimer von Hemmoor*, 1901, p. 213, and *Neue Untersuchungen über die römische Bronzeindustrie*, 1907, p. 69).

[34]

I have to thank Mr. W. M. Egglestone, of Stanhope, for information and for rubbings of the stamps. The E in the first stamp seems clear on the rubbing; all other examples have here I · or I. In the second stamp, the conclusion might be BI ·F. The *graffito* was first read INVINDA; it is, however, certainly as given above.

(8) Found at Holt, eight miles south of Chester (see above, p. 15), in the autumn of 1914, built upside down into the outer wall of a kiln, a centurial stone of the usual size and character, 10 inches long, 7-8 inches high, with letters (3/4-1 inch tall) inside a rude label

ƆCESo

NIANA

c(enturia) C(a)esoniana, set up by the century under Caesonius.

Like another centurial stone found some time ago at Holt (Eph. Epigr. ix. 1035), this was not found *in situ*; the kiln or other structure into the wall of which it was originally inserted must have been pulled down and its stones used up again.

The centuries mentioned would of course be units from the Twentieth Legion at Chester.

(9) Found at Holt late in 1914, a fragment of tile (about 7 × 7 inches) with parts of two (or three) lines of writing scratched on it.

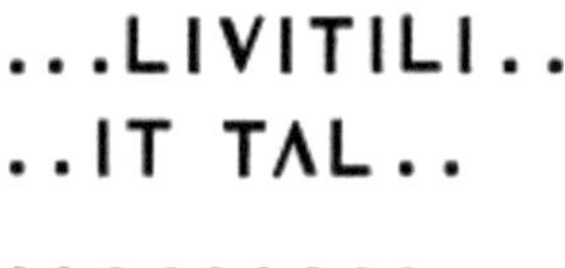

I can offer no guess at the sense of this. The third line may be mere scratches. I am indebted to Mr. Arthur Acton for sending Nos. 8 and 9 to me for examination.

(10) Found at Lincoln in 1906, on the site of the Technical Schools extensions (outside the east wall of the lower Roman town), a fragment from the lower right-hand corner of an inscribed slab flanked with foliation, 13 inches tall, 19 inches wide, with 2-inch lettering.

<table>
<tr><td>G</td><td>fol-</td></tr>
<tr><td>IND</td><td>iat-</td></tr>
<tr><td></td><td>ion.</td></tr>
</table>

No doubt one should prefix L to IND. That is, the inscription ended with some part of the Romano-British name of Lincoln, Lindum, or of its adjective Lindensis. From the findspot it seems probable that the inscription may have been sepulchral.

I am indebted to Mr. Arthur Smith, Curator of the City and County Museum at Lincoln, for a squeeze. The stone is now in the Museum.

[35]

(11) Found in London near the General Post Office in a rubbish-pit (see above, p. 23), two pieces of wood from the staves of a barrel which seems to have served as lining to a pit or well. They bear faint impressions of a metal stamp; (*a*) is repeated twice.

(*a*) EC · PACA . . . *and* . . C · PA . . †

(b) **CS**_or_ **CB**

The first stamp seems to include a name in the genitive, perhaps *Pacati*, but I do not know what TEC means.

(12) Found in another rubbish-pit of the same site as No. 11, a plain gold ring with three sunk letters on the bezel:

$$Q \cdot D \cdot D$$

Presumably the initials of an owner. The letters were at first read O ·D ·D, but the tail of the Q is discernible.

I am indebted to the Post Office authorities and to Mr. F. Lambert for a sight of Nos. 11 and 12. The objects are preserved at the General Post Office.

(13) I add here a note on a Roman milestone found in 1694 near Appleby and lately refound.

Among the papers of the antiquary Richard Gough in the Bodleian Library — more exactly, in his copy of Horsley's *Britannia*, gen. top. 128 = MS. 17653, fol. 44 *v.* — is recorded the text of a milestone of the Emperor Philip and his son, 'dug out of ye military way 1694, now at Hangingshaw'. The entry is written in Gough's own hand on the last page of a list of Roman and other inscriptions once belonging to Reginald Bainbridge, who was schoolmaster in Appleby in Elizabeth's reign and died there in 1606. 8 This list had been drawn up by one Hayton, under-schoolmaster at Appleby, in 1722 and had been copied out by Gough. There is, however, nothing to show whether the milestone, found eighty-eight years after the death of Bainbridge and plainly none of his collection, was added by Hayton, or was otherwise obtained by Gough and copied by him on a casually blank page; there is nothing even to connect either the stone or Hangingshaw with Appleby.

The notice lay neglected till Hübner undertook to edit the Roman inscriptions of Britain, which he issued in the seventh volume of the *Corpus Inscriptionum Latinarum* in 1873. He included the milestone as No. 1179. But, with his too frequent carelessness — a carelessness which makes the seventh volume of the *Corpus* far less valuable than the rest of the series—he christened the stone, in defiance of dates, [36] No. 17 in Bainbridge's collection; he also added the statement (which we shall see to be wrong) that Hangingshaw was near Old Carlisle. Fortunately, in the autumn of 1914, Mr. Percival Ross, the Yorkshire archaeologist, sent me a photograph of an inscription which he had come upon, built into the wall of a farm called Hangingshaw, about 200 yards from the Roman road which runs along the high ground a little east of Appleby. It then became plain—despite Hübner's errors—that this stone was that recorded in Gough's papers, although his copy was in one point faulty and on the other hand some letters which were visible in 1694 have now apparently perished. A rubbing sent me by the late Rev. A. Warren of Old Appleby helped further; I now give from the three sources— Gough's copy, the photograph, and the rubbing—what I hope may be a fairly accurate text. I premise that the letters RCO in line 2, LIPPO in 3, PHILIPPO in 8, IMO in 9, and I in 10 seem to be no longer visible but depend on Gough's copy.

IMPCΛⅭ
SΛRIMARCO
IVⅬIOPHILIPPO
PIOFEⅬICI
INVICTO
AVɊVSTO
*p*ERP
ETMIVLPHILIPPO
NOBILISSIMO
CΛESΛRI

The chief fault in Gough's copy is the omission of line 6, *Augusto*. This misled Hübner into treating line 7 (ERP) as a blundered reading of that necessary word. In reality, line 7 is the most interesting item in the inscription. It shows that the Emperor Philip was, here at least, styled *perpetuus Augustus*. That is an appellation to which I find no exact parallel in Philip's other inscriptions or indeed in any other imperial inscriptions till half a century after his death. It fits, however, into a definite development of the Roman imperial titles. In the earliest Empire, phrases occur, mostly on coins, such as *Aeternitas imperii* or *Aeternitas populi romani*. Soon the notion of the stability of the Empire was transferred to its rulers. As early as Vespasian, coins bear the legend *aeternitas Augusti*, and in the first years of the second century Pliny, writing to Trajan, speaks of petitions addressed *per salutem tuam aeternitatemque* and of 'works worthy of the emperor's eternity,' [37] (*opera aeternitate tua digna*). Late in the second century such phrases become commoner. With Severus Alexander (A.D. 221-35) coins begin to show the legend *Perpetuitas Aug.*, and before very long the indirect and abstract language changes into direct epithets which are incorporated in the emperors' titulature. The first case which I can find of this is that before us, of Philip (A.D. 244-9); a little later, Aurelian (A.D. 270-5) is styled *semper Augustus* and, from Diocletian onwards, *aeternus*, *perpetuus*, and *semper Augustus* belong to the customary titulature. Constantine I, for example, is called on one stone *invictus et perpetuus ... semper Augustus*, on another *perpetuus imperator, semper Augustus*. That Philip should have been the first to have applied to him, even once, the direct epithet, is probably a mere accident. One might have wished to connect it with his Secular Games, celebrated in 248. But by that time his son was no longer Caesar but full Augustus (since 246), and our stone must fall into the years 244-6.

The ideas underlying these epithets were perhaps mixed. Notions of or prayers for the long life of the Empire, the stability of the reigning house, the long reign of the current emperor, may have jostled with notions of the immortality of the emperors and their deification, and with the eastern ideas which poured into Rome as the second century ended and the third century began. 9 The hardening despotism of the imperial constitution, growing more and more autocratic every decade, also helped. As the emperor became unchecked and unqualified monarch, his appellations grew more emphatic; *perpetuus Augustus, semper Augustus* connoted that unchecked and autocratic rule.

C. PUBLICATIONS RELATING TO ROMAN BRITAIN IN 1914

The following summary of the books and articles on Roman Britain which appeared in 1914 is grouped under two heads, first, those few which deal with general aspects of the subject, and secondly, the far larger number which concern special sites or areas. In this second class, those which belong to England are placed under their counties in alphabetical order, while those which belong to Wales and Scotland are grouped under these two headings. I have in general admitted only matter which was published in 1914, or which bears that date.

1. General

(1) Mr. G. L. Cheesman's *Auxilia of the Roman Imperial Army* (Oxford University Press) does not deal especially with Roman Britain, but it deserves brief notice here. It is an excellent and up-to-date sketch of an important section of the Roman army, with which British archaeologists are much concerned. It also contains valuable lists, which can be found nowhere else, of the 'auxiliary' regiments stationed in Britain (pp. 146-9 and 170-1). It is full, cheap, compact; every historical and archaeological library should get it.

(2) A learned and scholarly attempt to settle the obscure chronology of the north British frontiers in the fourth century has been made by Mr. H. Craster, Fellow of All Souls, and one of the excavators of Corbridge, in the *Archaeological Journal* (lxxi. 25-44). His conclusions are novel and, though to some extent disputable, are well worth printing. Starting from the known fact that, during much of the third century, the north frontier of Roman Britain coincided roughly with the line of Cheviot and was then withdrawn to the line of Hadrian's Wall, he distinguishes five stages in the subsequent history. (1) At or just before the outset of the fourth century, in the reign of Diocletian, the Wall was reorganized in some ill-recorded fashion. (2) Thirty years later, towards the end of Constantine's reign, about A.D. 320-30, it was (he thinks) further reorganized; perhaps its mile-castles were then discarded. (3) Thirty or forty years later still, [39] after disturbances which (he conjectures) included the temporary loss of Hadrian's Wall and the destruction of its garrisons, Theodosius carried out in 369 a fuller reorganization. This garrison had consisted of the regiments known to us by various evidence as posted 'per lineam valli' in the third and early fourth centuries; their places were now filled by soldiers of whom we know absolutely nothing. (4) In 383 Maximus withdrew these unknown troops for his continental wars. Now perhaps the line of the Wall had to be given up, but Tyne and Solway, South Shields, Corbridge, and Carlisle were still held. (5) Finally, about 395-9, Stilicho ordered a last reorganization; he withdrew the frontier from the Tyne to the Tees, from Carlisle to Lancaster, and garrisoned the new line with new soldiery—those, namely, which are listed in the Notitia as serving under the Dux Britanniarum, save only the regi-

ments 'per lineam valli'; these last the compiler of the Notitia borrowed from the older order to disguise the loss of the Wall. Even this did not last. In 402 Stilicho had to summon troops to Italy for home defence—among them, Mr. Craster suggests, the Sixth Legion—and in 407 the remaining Roman soldiers, including the Second Legion, were taken to the continent by Constantine III.

Every one who handles this difficult period must indulge in conjecture; Mr. Craster has, perhaps, indulged rather much. It might be simpler to connect the abandonment of the mile-castles—his stage 2—with the recorded troubles which called Constans to Britain in 343, rather than invent an unrecorded action by Constantine I. I hesitate also to assume for the period 369-83 an otherwise unknown frontier garrison, which has left no trace of itself. I feel still greater doubt respecting the years 383-99. Here Mr. Craster argues from coin-finds. No coins have been found on the line of the Wall which were minted later than 383, and none at Corbridge, Carlisle, and South Shields which were minted later than 395; therefore, he infers, the Wall was abandoned soon after 383, and the other sites soon after 395. This is too rigid an argument. It may be a mere accident that the Wall has as yet yielded no coin which was minted between 383 and 395. At Wroxeter, for example, two small hoards were found some years ago which had clearly been lost at the moment when the town was sacked. By these hoards we should be able to date the catastrophe. Now the latest coin in one hoard was minted in or before 377, and the latest in the other in or before 383. But newer finds show that Wroxeter was not destroyed at earliest till after 390. Again, as Mr. Craster himself says, the coining of Roman copper practically stopped in 395; after that year the older copper [40] issues appear to have remained in use for many a long day. That is clear in Gaul, where coins later than 395 seem to be rare, although Roman armies and influences were present for another fifty years. When Mr. Craster states that 'archaeology gives no support to the theory that the Tyne-Solway line was held after 395', he might add that it gives equally little support to the theory that it was not held after 395.

Incidentally, he offers a new theory of the two chapters in the Notitia Dignitatum which describe the forces commanded by the Comes Litoris Saxonici and the Dux Britanniarum (*Occ.* 28 and 40).

It is agreed that these chapters do not exhibit the garrison of Britain at the moment when the Notitia was substantially completed, about A.D. 425, for the good reason that there was then no garrison left in the island; they exhibit some garrison which had then ceased to exist, and which is mentioned, apparently, to disguise the loss of the province. The question is, to what date do they refer? Mommsen long ago pointed out that the regiments enumerated in one part of them (the 'per lineam valli' section) are very much the same as existed in the third century. Seeck added the suggestion that these regiments remained in garrison till 383, when Maximus marched them off to the continent. According to him, the garrison of the Wall through the first eighty years of the fourth century was much the same as it had been in the third century, with certain changes and additions. Mr. Craster holds a different view. He thinks that most of the troops named in these chapters were due to Stilicho's reorganization in 395-9, but that one section, headed 'per lineam valli', records troops who had been in Britain in the third century and had been destroyed before 369. I cannot feel that he has proved his case. One would have thought that, when the compiler of the Notitia in 425 wanted to fill the gap left by the loss of the Wall, he would have gone back to the last garrison of the Wall, that is, on Mr. Craster's view, the garrison of 369-83, not to arrangements which had vanished some years earlier. But the problems of this obscure period are not to be solved without many attacks. We must be glad that Mr. Craster has delivered a serious attack; even if he has not succeeded, his scholarly discussion may make things easier for the next assailants.

(3) The *Antiquary* for 1914 contains an attempt by Mr. W. J. Kaye to catalogue all the examples of triple vases of Roman date found in Britain. It also prints a note by myself (p. 439) on the topography of the campaign of Suetonius against Boudicca, which argues that the defeat of the British warrior queen occurred somewhere on Watling Street between Chester (or Wroxeter) and London.

Fig. 18. Tile Graves in the Infirmary Field, Chester

[41]

(4) In the *Sitzungsberichte der kgl. preuss. Akademie* (1914, p. 635), prof. Kuno Meyer, late of Liverpool, argues that the Celtic name of St. Patrick, commonly spelt Sucat and explained as akin to Celtic words meaning 'brave in war' (stem *su-*, 'good'), ought to be really spelt Succet and connected with Gaulish names like Succius and Sucelus. This, he thinks, destroys the last remnant of a reason for Zimmer's idea that Patrick was the same as Palladius.

2. Special Sites or Districts

Berks

(5) Some notes of traces, near Kintbury west of Speen (Spinae), of the Roman road from Silchester to Bath are given by Mr. O. G. S. Crawford in the *Berks, Bucks, and Oxon Archaeological Journal* for Oct. 1914 (xx. 96).

Cheshire

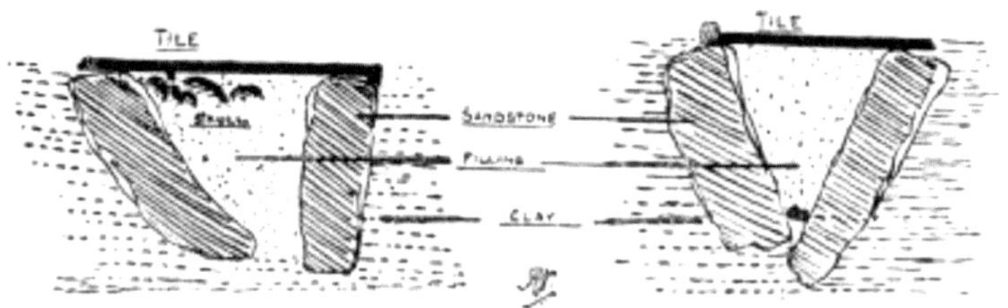

Fig. 17. Graves in the Infirmary Field, Chester

(6) In *Annals of Archaeology and Anthropology* (Liverpool, 1914, vol. vi, pp. 121-67) Prof. Newstead describes and illustrates fully the thirty-five graves found in 1912-3 in the Infirmary Field, Chester, of which I gave a brief account in my Report for 1913 (p. 14). Save for a few first-century remains in one corner, the graveyard seems to be an inhumation cemetery, used during the second half of the second century—rather an early date for such a cemetery. I do not myself feel much doubt that some at least of the tombstones extracted in 1890-2 from the western half of the North City Wall were taken from this area. They belong to the first and second centuries and suggest (as I pointed out when they were found) that the Wall was built about A.D. 200. That, however, is just the date when the cemetery was closed; the seizure of the tombstones for the construction of the Wall would explain why the Infirmary Field has yielded no tombstones from all its graves. By the kindness of [42] Professors Bosanquet and Newstead I can add some illustrations of the graves themselves, from blocks used for Prof. Newstead's paper. Fig. 17 shows two of the simpler graves, fig. 18, two built with tiles. Fig. 19 illustrates some curious nails found with the bodies.

(7) A list of the place-names of Derbyshire with philological notes is commenced by Mr. B. Walker, sometime of Liverpool University, in the *Proceedings of the Derbyshire Archaeological and Natural History Society* for 1913 (xxxvi. 123-284, Derby, 1914); it is to be completed in a future volume. I venture two suggestions. First, like, many similar treatises on place-names which are now being issued, this work has too limited a scope. It deals mainly with certain names of modern towns and villages; it takes little or no heed of ancient names of houses and fields or of lanes and roads (as Bathamgate, Doctorgate), or of rivers (as Noe), or (lastly) of the place-names of the older England which are preserved only in charters, chronicles, and the like; unless they chance to come among the select list of modern names which the writer chooses to admit, they find no notice. Yet it is the older names of all sorts, irrespective of their survival in prominent fashion to-day, with which historical students and even philologists are most really concerned. Secondly, writers on place-names take too little account of facts outside the phonetic horizon. In the present instalment of Derbyshire, the one Roman item noted is Derby. Here, in the suburb of Little Chester, was a Roman fort or village, and past it flows the river then and now called Derwent or something similar. Yet the etymology of Derby is discussed without any reference to the river name. No doubt Derby is not derived by regular phonetic process from Derwent; its earliest spellings, Deoraby and the like, connect it with either the word for 'wild beast' or the proper name Deor. Still, it is incredible that the Derwent should flow past Derby and the adjacent Darley (formerly Derley) and be unrelated. One may guess with little rashness that the invaders who renamed the site took over the Romano-British name (Deruentio or the like) and reshaped that after analogies of their own speech. Does not a form Deorwenta occur (though Mr. Walker has missed it) to show that the two names interacted? Again, Chesterfield (Cesterfelda, A.D. 955) is glossed as 'the field by the fort'. What fort? There is none, nor does 'Chester' necessarily mean that there was. Etymologizing without reference to facts is wasted work.

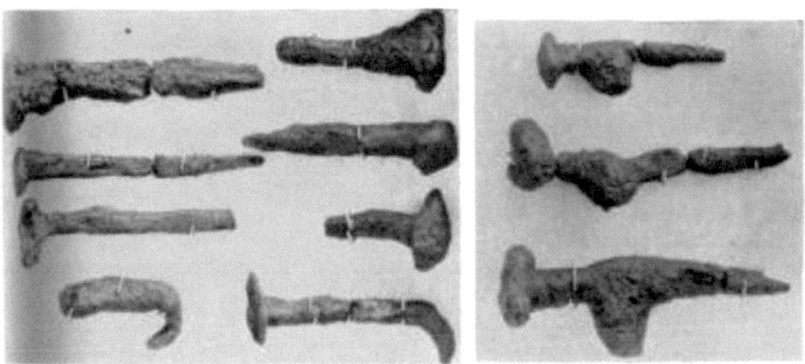

Fig. 19. Nails from the Chester Graves. (p. 42)

Fig. 20. The Mersea Grave Mound. (p. 43)

Fig. 21. Leaden Casket and Glass Sepulchral Vessel from the Mersea
Burial-Mound. (p. 43)

[43]

Dorset

(8) In the *Numismatic Chronicle* for 1914 (pp. 92-5), Mr. H. Symonds lists 107 'third brass' from a hoard found (it seems) about 1850 near Puncknoll. They consist of 3 Gallienus, 2 Salonina, 55 Postumus, 40 Victorinus, 3 Tetricus, 1 Tetricus junior, 2 Claudius Gothicus, and 1 Garausius. The hoard was, then, of a familiar type; its original size we cannot guess. A brief reference to the same hoard occurs in the *Proceedings of the Dorset Natural History and Antiquarian Field Club* (xxxv, p. li).

(9) The latter periodical (pp. 88, 118) also contains Mr. H. Gray's Fifth Report on the gradual exploration of the Roman amphitheatre and the underlying prehistoric remains at Maumbury Rings, Dorchester—now substantially concluded—and an interesting little note on the New Forest pottery-works by Mr. Sumner (p. xxxii).

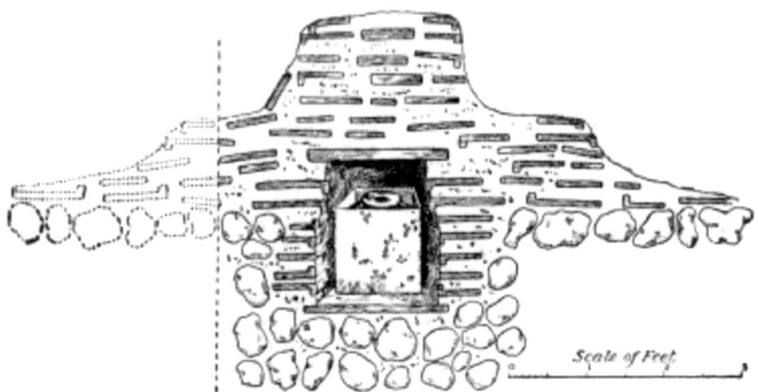

Fig. 22. Restoration of the tile-built grave-chamber of the Mersea
Mound

(10) By the kindness of the Morant Club and the Essex Archaeological Society, I am able to reproduce here three illustrations of the
finds in the Mersea Mound, which I mentioned in my Report for
1913 (p. 42). Figs. 20, 22 show a view of the actual tomb; fig. 21
shows the chief contents. The interest of these half-native, half-
Roman grave-mounds, which occur in eastern Britain and in the
Low Countries opposite, will justify their insertion here. I may also
correct an error in my account. No 'Samian stamped VITALIS' [44]
was found at Mersea, but objects which have been elsewhere found
in association with that stamp.

(11) Two small Essex excavations are recorded in the *Transactions
of the Essex Archaeological Society*, vol. xiii. At Chadwell St. Mary,
near Tilbury, Mr. Miller Christy and Mr. F. W. Reader explored an
early-looking mound, only to find that it was probably mediaeval
(pp. 218-33). At Hockley, also in South Essex, the same archaeologists with Mr. E. B. Francis dug into a similar mound and met with
many potsherds of Roman date and a coin of Domitian; no trace of a
burial was detected, such as has come to light in other Romano-
British mounds at Mersea, Bartlow, and elsewhere (*ibid.*, p. 224).
Indeed, it does not seem quite clear that the mound was thrown up

in Roman times; it may have been reared later, with earth which contained Romano-British objects.

Gloucester

(12) The *Transactions of the Bristol and Gloucestershire Archaeological Society* (vol. xxxvi) refers to excavations at Sea Mills, on the King's Weston estate, in February 1913; the finds appear not to have been extensive. They also record the transfer of the Roman 'villa' at Witcombe to the care of H.M. Office of Works by the owner, Mr. W. F. Hicks-Beach.

Hants

(13) Mr. Heywood Sumner's pamphlet *Excavations on Rockbourne Down* (London, 1914, p. 43) is a readable, scholarly, and well-illustrated account of a Romano-British farm-site five miles south-west of Salisbury on the edge of Cranborne Chase. Mr. Sumner excavated parts of it in 1911-13; his account appeared so early in 1914 that it found a place in my Report for 1913 (pp. 23-5).

(14) Some Roman roads in Hampshire are treated in the *Papers and Proceedings of the Hampshire Field Club and Archaeological Society* (vii, part 1). Capt. G. A. Kempthorne writes on the road east and west of Silchester and Mr. Karslake adds a word as to the line outside the west gate of that town, which he puts north of the generally assumed line (p. 25). Mr. O. G. S. Crawford and Mr. J. P. Freeman-Williams deal with very much more uncertain roads in the New Forest—one across Beaulieu Heath, another from Otterbourn to Ringwood (pp. 34-42).

(15) Mr. Karslake also (*ibid.*, p. 43) notes that the outer entrenchment [45] at Silchester, which is thought to be pre-Roman, does not coincide with the south-eastern front of the Roman town-walls, as we have all supposed, but runs as much as 300 yards outside them.

Herefordshire

See p. 62, below.

Herts

(16) Mr. Urban A. Smith, the Herts County Surveyor, submitted in 1912 to his County Council a Report on the Roman roads of the county, which is now printed in the *Transactions of the East Herts*

Archaeological Society (v. 117-31). It deals mainly with the surviving traces of these roads and the question of preserving them in public use. The roads selected as Roman are by no means all certain or probable Roman roads. The article is furnished with a map, which however omits several names used in the text.

Kent

(17) A few notes on the Roman Pharos at Dover and on some un-explained pits near it, by Lieut. Peck, R.E., are given in the *Journal of the British Archaeological Association* (xx. 248 foll.).

(18) In the *Transactions of the Greenwich Antiquarian Society* (vol. i, parts 3, 4) Mr. J. M. Stone and Mr. J. E. de Montmorency write on the line which the Roman road from Dover and Canterbury to London followed near Greenwich. Its course is quite clear as far west as the outskirts of Greenwich; thence it is doubtful all the way to London. In these papers evidence is advanced that a piece of road was closed in the lower part of Greenwich Park in 1434 and it is suggested that this was a bit of the lost Roman line. If so, the road ran straight on from Shooter's Hill, across Greenwich Park and the site of the Hospital School, towards the mouth of Deptford Creek. It is, however, hard to see how it crossed that obstacle, or why it should have run so near the Thames at this point, where the shore must have been very marshy.

Lancashire

(19) In the *Transactions of the Lancashire and Cheshire Antiquarian Society* (xxxi. 69-87) Mr. W. Harrison discusses the Roman road which runs from Ribchester to Overborough for twenty-seven lonely miles through the hills of north-east Lancashire. He does not profess to add to our knowledge of the line of the road; he directs [46] attention rather to the reasons for the course which the road pursues, its diversions from the straight line, and its gradients. He notes also, as others have noted, the absence of any intermediate fort half-way along the twenty-seven miles. Probably there was such a fort; but it must have stood in the wildest part of the road, almost in the heart of the Forest of Bowland and perhaps somewhere in Croasdale, and it has never been detected. The greater ease of the lowland route from Ribchester by Lancaster to Overborough may have led to the early abandonment of the shorter mountain

track and of any post which guarded its central portion. That, at any rate, is the suggestion which I would offer to Lancashire antiquaries as a working hypothesis.

(20) In the same journal Mr. J. W. Jackson lists some animal remains found among the Roman remains of Manchester (pp. 113-18).

Lincolnshire

(21) Samian fragments, mostly of the second century but including shape '29', found in making new streets and sewers in Lincoln, are noted in *Lincolnshire Notes and Queries*, xiii. 1-4.

(22) In south Lincolnshire, between Ulceby and Dexthorpe, chance excavation has revealed tiles, potsherds, iron nails, and a few late coins (Victorinus-Constantine junior, nob. caes.) on a site which has previously yielded Roman scraps (*ibid.*, p. 34). The tiles point to some sort of farm or other dwelling.

London

(23) In his new volume *London* (London, 1914) Sir L. Gomme continues his efforts to prove that English London can trace direct and uninterrupted descent from Roman Londinium. Though, he says (p. 9), 'Roman civilization certainly ceased in Britain with the Anglo-Saxon conquest, ... amidst the wreckage London was able to continue its use of the Roman city constitution in its new position as an English city'. I can only record my conviction that not all his generous enthusiasm provides proof that Roman London survived the coming of the English. The root-error in his arguments is perhaps a failure to realize the Roman side of the argument. He says, for instance, that, though not a 'colonia', Londinium had the rank of 'municipium civium Romanorum'. There is not the least reason to think that it was a 'municipium'. So again, his references to a 'botontinus' on Hampstead Heath (p. 86), to the 'jurisdictional [47] terminus' of Roman London at Mile End (p. 95), to its 'pomerium' (p. 98), its right of forming commercial alliances with other cities, which 'lasted into the Middle Ages and is a direct survival of the system adopted in Roman towns' (p. 101), its position as a 'city-state' and its relation to the choice of Emperors (pp. 105, 130)—all this has nothing to do with the real Londinium; these things did not exist in the Roman town. When Sir Laurence goes on to assert that 'the ritual of

St. Paul's down to the seventeenth century preserved the actual rites of the worship of Diana', he again falls short of proof. What part of the ritual and what rites of Diana? 10

(24) In the December number of the *Journal of the British Archaeological Association* (xx. 307) Mr. F. Lambert, of the Guildhall Museum, prints pertinent criticisms of Sir L. Gomme's volume, much in the direction of my preceding paragraphs. He also makes useful observations on Roman London. In particular, he attacks the difficult problem of the date when its town-walls were built. Here he agrees with those who ascribe them to the second century, and for two main reasons. First, he thinks that the occurrence of early Roman potsherds at certain points near the walls proves the town to have grown to its full extent by about A.D. 100. Secondly, he points to the foundations of the Roman gate at Newgate; as they are shallower than those of the adjacent town-walls, he dates the gate after the walls and thus obtains (as he hopes) an early date for the walls. Both points were worth raising, but I doubt if either proves Mr. Lambert's case. For (*a*) the potsherds come mostly from groups of rubbish-pits—such as those which Mr. Lambert himself has lately done good work in helping to explore—and rubbish-pits, especially in groups, lie rather outside the inhabited areas of towns. Those of London itself suggest to me that the place had *not* reached its full area by A.D. 100 (see above, p. 23). (*b*) The Newgate foundations are harder to unravel. As a rule, Roman town-gates had large superstructures and needed stronger foundations than the town-walls. At Newgate, where the superstructure must have been comparatively slender, the published plans show that under a part, at least, of the gate-towers the undisturbed subsoil rises higher than beneath the adjacent town-walls. According to the elevation published by Dr. Norman and Mr. F. W. Reader in *Archaeologia* lxiii, plate lvii, the wall-builders at this point stopped their deep foundation trenches [48] for the full width of the gateway (98 feet), or at least dug them shallower there. No motive for such action could be conceived except the wish to leave a passage for a gate. There would seem, therefore, to have been an entrance into Roman London at Newgate as early as the building of the walls, and there may have been such an entrance even before the erection of these walls. Dr. Norman has, however, warned me that plate lvii goes much beyond the actual

evidence (see plate lvi); practically, we do not know enough to form conjectures of any value on this point.

(25) In the *Journal of the Royal Institute of British Architects* for April 11, 1914 (xxi. 333), Mr. W. R. Davidge prints a lecture on the Development of London which deals mostly with present and future London but also contains a new theory as to the Roman town. Hitherto, most writers have agreed that, while Londinium may have been laid out on a regular town-plan, no discoverable trace of such plan survived, nor could any existing street be said to run to any serious extent on Roman lines. Mr. Davidge devises a rectangular plan of oblong blocks, and finds vestiges of Roman streets in the present Cheapside, Cannon Street, Gracechurch Street, and Birchin Lane. In a later number of the same journal (Aug. 29, p. 52) I have given some reasons for not accepting this view. First, Mr. Davidge's list of four survivals would be too brief to prove much if the survivals were proved. Secondly, Roman structural remains seem to have been found under all the streets in question, and it is, therefore, plain that they do not run on the lines of Roman thoroughfares. Thirdly, his suggested plan brings none of his conjectured Roman streets (except one) to any of the various known gates of Londinium; it requires us to assume a number of other gates for which there is neither probability nor proof.

(26) In the Post Office Magazine, *St. Martin's-le-Grand* (Jan. and July 1914), Mr. Thos. Wilson, then Clerk of the Works, gives details, with illustrations, of the Roman rubbish-pits lately excavated at the General Post Office (see above, p. 23).

Norfolk

(27) In the earlier pages (1-45) of his *Roman Camp at Burgh Castle* (London, 1913) Mr. L. H. Dahl deals with the Roman fort at Burgh Castle (Gariannonum), near Yarmouth, which formed part of the fourth-century *Litus Saxonicum*. His account, which is not very technical, seems based on previous writers, Ives, Harrod, Fox. I note [49] a list of thirty coins which, save for an uncertain specimen of Domitian and one of Marcus, belong entirely to the late third and the fourth centuries, and end with two silver of Honorius (*Virtus Romanorum*, Cohen 59). He detects a Roman road running east from Burgh Castle towards Gorleston, preserved (he thinks) in an old

road sometimes called the Jews' Way; this, however, seems unlikely. He also maintains the view, which others have held, that the fort had no defences towards the water. This again seems unlikely. Burgh Castle, like Richborough, Stutfall, and other forts of the *Litus*, may well have had different arrangements on its water-front from the walls on its other three faces. But it cannot have lacked defences, and excavations prove, here as elsewhere, that walls did actually exist on this side.

Northumberland: Corbridge

(28) A paper by the present writer and Prof. P. Gardner, entitled 'Roman silver in Northumberland' (*Journal of Roman Studies*, iv. 1-12), discusses the relics of what was seemingly a hoard — or perhaps a service — of Roman silver plate, lost in the Tyne or on its banks near Corbridge in the fourth century. Of five pieces, four were picked up between 1731 and 1736, about 100-150 yards below the present bridge at Corbridge; a fifth was found in 1760 floating in the stream four miles lower down. One was a silver 'basin', of which no more is recorded. Another was a small two-handled cup with figures of men and beasts round it. A third was a round flat-bottomed bowl, with a decorated rim bearing the Chi-Rho amidst its other ornament. A fourth was a small ovoid cup, 4 inches high, with the inscription *Desideri vivas*. Last, not least, is the Corbridge Lanx, the only surviving piece of the five, and probably the finest piece of Roman engraved silver found in these islands, an oblong dish measuring 15 × 19 inches, weighing 148 ounces, and ornamented with figures of deities from classical mythology. That all five pieces belonged together can hardly be doubted, though it cannot be proved outright. That they all belong to the later Roman period, and probably to the fourth century, seems highly probable. Whether they were buried in the river-bank to conceal them from raiders or were lost from a boat or otherwise, is not now discoverable. But the occurrence of such silver close to the Roman Wall is in itself notable. It is to be attributed rather to a Roman officer residing in or passing through Corbridge than to either a Romanized Briton or a Pictish looter.

Apart from its findspot, the Lanx is important for its excellent [50] art and for the place which it seems to hold in the history of later

Greek art. It is, of course, not Romano-British work; it is purely Greek in all its details and no doubt of Greek workmanship. The deities figured on it have long been a puzzle. They are evidently classical deities; three of them, indeed, are Apollo, Artemis, and Athena. But the identity of the other two figures and the meaning of the whole scene have been much disputed. Roger Gale, the first to attempt its unravelment, suggested in 1735 that it was 'just an assemblage of deities', and at one time I inclined to this view — that we had here merely (let us say) a tea-party at Apollo's; Dr. Drexel, too, wrote to me lately to express the same idea. But I must confess that nearly all the best archaeologists demand a definite mythological identification, and my colleague, Prof. Gardner, suggests a new view — that the scene is the so-called Judgement of Paris. This mythological incident was often depicted in ancient art, and — strange as it may sound — in the later versions Paris was not seldom omitted, Apollo was made arbiter, and the scene was removed from Mount Ida to Delphi. 11 The two hitherto disputable figures are, Prof. Gardner thinks, Hera (seated) and Aphrodite (standing, with a long sceptre). He ascribes the work to the third or early part of the fourth century, and believes that it was made in the Eastern Empire; from the prominence granted to Artemis, he conjectures that Ephesus may have been its origin. But he adds that he would not be sure that the artist of the piece, while copying a Judgement of Paris, was consciously aware of the meaning of the original before him. His views will be published in fuller detail in the *Journal of Hellenic Studies*.

I am glad, further, to have been able to illustrate this paper by what I believe to be a better illustration of the Lanx than has been published before, and also to set out in more accurate fashion the curious legal history of the object after it was found.

(29) In the new *History of Northumberland*, issued by the Northumberland County History Committee in vol. x (edited by Mr. H. H. Craster, Newcastle, 1914, pp. 455-522) I have given a long account of the known Roman remains in Corbridge parish. These are the settlement of Corstopitum, a small stretch of Roman road and another of the Roman Wall, and the fort of Halton (Hunnum) on the Wall. The account is necessarily historical rather than archaeological; it tries to sum up the finds and estimate their historical bearing, and it also catalogues all the inscribed and sculptured stones found

at Corbridge and Halton, with the 'literature' relating to [51] them. Mr. Knowles contributes a plan of the Corbridge excavations to the end of 1912.

(30) The Corbridge excavations of 1913 are described by Mr. R. H. Forster, who was in personal charge of the work, Mr. W. H. Knowles, and myself, in *Archaeologia Aeliana* (third series, 1914, xi. 279-310); see also a short account by myself in the *Proceedings of the Society of Antiquaries of London* (xxvi. 185-9). The discoveries were comparatively few; they comprised some ill-preserved and mostly insignificant buildings on the north side of the site, some ditches, and a stretch of the road leading to the north (Dere Street). Among small objects were an interesting but imperfect altar to 'Panthea ...', a bronze 'balsamarium' showing a puzzling variety of barbarian's head, and another piece of the Corbridge grey *appliqué* ware. A short account of the excavations of 1914 (see above, p. 9) is contained in the *Journal of the British Archaeological Association* (xx. 343).

(31) The *Proceedings of the Berwick Naturalists' Club* (vol. xxxii, part 2) print an agreeable paper by Mr. James Curle, describing Dere Street and some Roman posts on it between Tyne and Tweed.

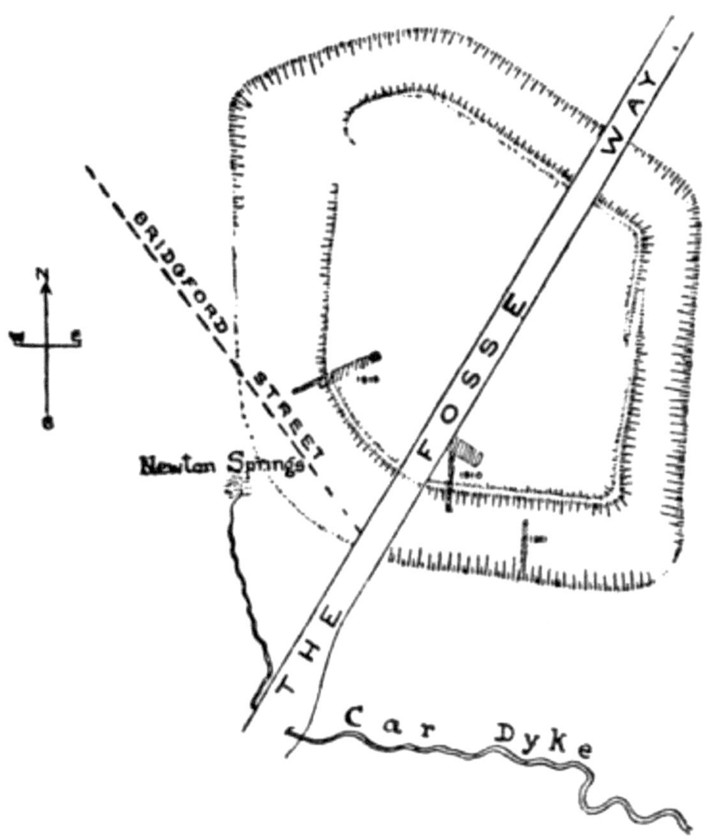

Fig. 23. Roman Site near East Bridgeford, Notts. (No. 32)

Fig. 24. Decoration of Enamelled Seal-box.

(32) About ten miles east from Nottingham, and a mile south of the village of East Bridgeford, the Fosse-way crosses a Roman site which has usually been identified with the Margidunum of the [52] Antonine Itinerary. Lately excavation has been attempted, and the *Antiquary* of December 1914 contains an interesting account of the results attained up to the end of 1913, with some illustrations. 12 A very broad earthwork and ditch surround an area of 7 acres, rhomboidal in shape (fig. 23). In this area the excavators, Drs. Felix Oswald and T. D. Pryce, have turned up floor-tesserae, roof-slates, flue-tiles, window-glass, painted wall-plaster, potsherds of the first and later centuries, including a black bowl with a well-modelled figure of Mercury in relief, coins ranging down to the end of the fourth century (Eugenius), and other small objects of interest, such as the small seal-box with Late-Celtic enamel, shown in fig. 24. No foundations *in situ* have yet come to light, but that is doubtless to follow; only a tiny part of the whole area has, as yet, been touched. Margidunum may have begun as a fort coeval with the Fosse-way, which (if I am right) dates from the earliest years of the Roman Conquest. Whether any of the first-century potsherds as yet found there can be assigned to these years (say A.D. 45-75) is not clear. But the excavations plainly deserve to be continued.

Shropshire

(33) Mr. Bushe-Fox's second Report on his excavations at Wroxeter (*Reports of the Research Committee of the London Society of Antiquaries*, No. II, Oxford, 1914) deserves all the praise accorded to his first Report. I can only repeat what I said of that; it is an excellent de-

scription, full and careful, minute in its account of the smaller finds, lavishly illustrated, admirably printed, and sold for half a crown. The finds which it enumerates in detail I summarized in my Report for 1913, pp. 19-20 — the temple with its interesting Italian plan, the fragments of sculpture which seem to belong to it, the crowd of small objects, the masses of Samian (indefatigably recorded), the 528 coins; all combine to make up an admirable pamphlet.

I will venture a suggestion on the temple. This, as I pointed out last year, is on the Italian, not on the Celto-Roman plan. But one item is not quite clear in it. All ordinary classical temples stood on *podia* or platforms which raised them above the surrounding surface at least to some small extent. Mr. Bushe-Fox speaks of a *podium* to the Wroxeter temple. But it appears that he does not mean a *podium*, as generally understood. The masonry which he denotes by that term was, in his opinion, buried underground and merely foundation.

Fig. 27. The Podium, as seen from the north
(The measuring staff to the right stands in the *cella*, the floor of which is slightly higher than that of the portico to the left of it)

Fig. 28. East wall of Podium, coursed Masonry with Clay and Rubble Foundations

THE WROXETER TEMPLE. (p. 53)

[53]

The floor of the portico of the temple (he says) was about level with the floor of the court which surrounded the temple; the floor of the *cella*, though higher, was but a trifle higher (see figs. 26, 27). This view needs more reflection than he has given it in his rather brief account. No doubt a temple in a Celtic land might have been built on a classical plan, though without a classical *podium*. But it is not what one would most expect. Nor do I feel sure that it was actually done at Wroxeter in this case. The walls which Mr. Bushe-Fox explains as the foundations of the temple are quite needlessly good masonry for foundations never meant to be seen; this will be plain from figs. 27, 28, which I reproduce by permission from his Report. Further, as fig. 26 (from the same source) shows, there was outside the base of this masonry a level cobbled surface, for which no structural reason is to be found. This, one may guess, was a pavement at the original ground-level when the temple was first erected; from this, steps presumably led up to the floor of the portico and *cella*. The [54] 'podium', then, was at first a real *podium*. Later, the ground-level rose, and the walls of the *podium* were buried.

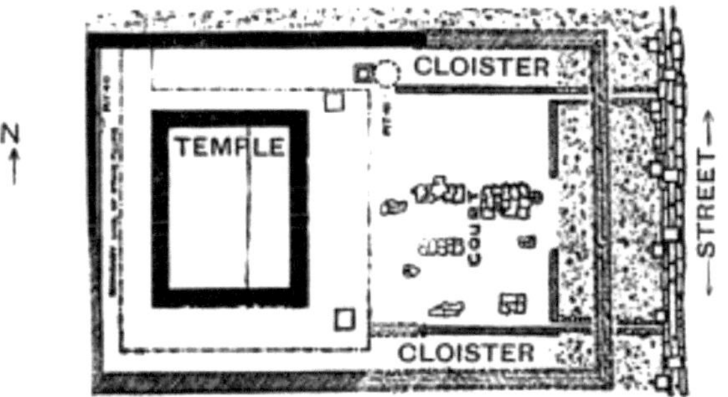

Fig. 25. Temple at Wroxeter

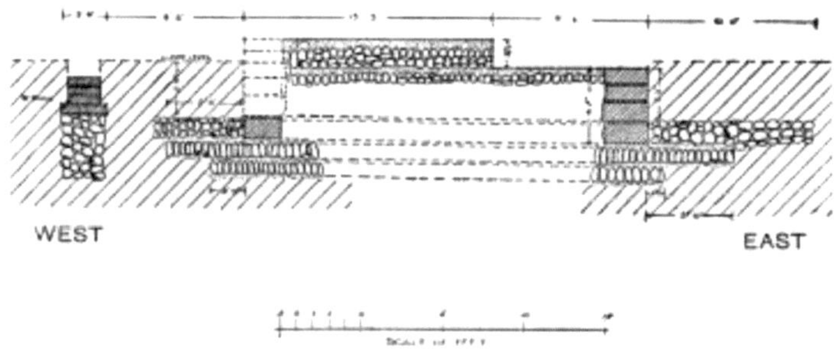

Fig. 26. Foundations of Wroxeter Temple

Somerset

(34) In his handsome volume, *Wookey Hole, its caves and cave-dwellers* (London, 1914), Mr. H. E. Balch collects for general antiquarian readers the results of his long exploration of this Mendip cave; some of these results were noted in my Report for 1913, p. 47. The cave, as a whole, contained—besides copious prehistoric remains—two well-defined Roman layers, with many potsherds, including a little Samian and one Samian stamp given as PIIR PIIT

OFII (apparently a new variety of Perpetuus), broken glass, a few fibulae and other bronze and iron objects, and 106 coins. These coins are:—1 Republican (124-103 B.C., Marcia), 1 Vespasian, 1 Titus, 1 Trajan, 2 Hadrian, 2 Pius; then, 3 Gallienus, 1 Salonina, 1 Carausius, 2 Chlorus, 1 Theodora, 6 Constantinopolis, 1 Crispus, 4 Constantine II, 4 Magnentius, 4 Constantius II, with 20 Valentinian I, 14 Valens, 21 Gratian, 7 Valentinian II, and 6 illegible. Just two-thirds of the coins are later than A.D. 364; they may be set beside the late hoard found at Wookey Hole in 1852, which Mr. Balch might well have mentioned. Plainly, the later Roman layer in the cave belongs to the end of the fourth century. The date of the other layer is harder to fix, since we are not told how the coins and potsherds were distributed between the layers. Probably the cave was long inhabited casually but in the troubled time of the latest Empire became a place of refuge or otherwise attracted more numerous occupants. That, if true, is a more interesting result that Mr. Balch realizes. For in general the cave-life of Roman Britain belonged to the first two or three centuries of our era; it is only rarely, and mostly in the west country, that the caves contain among their Roman relics objects of the late fourth century (see *Victoria Hist. Derbyshire*, i. 233-42). I must add that Mr. Balch repeats on pp. 57-8 the error about the significance of the Republican coin which was noted in my Report for 1915.

(35) The *Proceedings of the Somersetshire Archaeological and Natural History Society* for 1913 (vol. lix, Taunton, 1914) record small Roman finds at Bratton and Barrington (part i, pp. 24, 65, 76, and part ii, p. 79), and describe in detail Mr. Gray's trial excavations at Cadbury Castle. Cadbury, it seems, was occupied mainly in the Celtic period, before the Roman conquest.

(36) A little light is thrown on two Somerset 'villas' in *Notes and [55] Queries for Somerset and Dorset* (xiv. 1914). (*a*) Skinner in 1818 excavated a 'villa' near Camerton which he recorded in his manuscripts. (British Mus. Add. 33659, &c.) and which I described in print in the *Victoria History of Somerset* (i. 315). His account did not, however, enable one to fix the precise site; he said only that it stood south of a certain Ridgeway and next to a field called Chessils. Mr. E. J. Holmroyd has now, with the aid of tithe maps, discovered a field called Chessils in the north of Midsomer Norton parish, about a mile east of Paulton village, at the point where a lane called in the

Ordnance Survey 'Coldharbour Lane', which runs north and south, cuts a lane running east and west from Camerton to Paulton; this latter lane keeps to high ground and must be Skinner's Ridgeway. In Chessils and in adjoining fields called Cornwell, just 525 feet above sea-level, he has, further, actually found Roman potsherds, tiles, and rough tesserae. This, as he says (*Notes and Queries*, xiv. 5, and in a letter to me) will be the site of Skinner's 'villa.' (*b*) In the same publication (p. 122) I have pointed out that the Parish Award (1798) of Chedzoy, near Bridgwater, contains a field-name Chesters. This, as the Rector of Chedzoy attests, is still in use there, as the name of an orchard on the Manor Farm, just west of Chedzoy village. According to older statements, a hypocaust was long ago found in 'Slapeland', and Slapeland too lies west of Chedzoy village (see *Vict. Hist. Somerset*, i. 359). Two bits of slender evidence seem thus to confirm each other, although no actual Roman remains have been noted at Chedzoy lately.

(37) In the *Proceedings of the Society of Antiquaries of London* (xxvi. 137-44) Mr. A. Bulleid describes, with illustrations, some excavations which he lately made in the marshes north of the Polden Hills, near Cossington and Chilton. Here are curious mounds which have often been taken for some kind of potteries, and are so explained by Mr. Bulleid; many of these mounds were excavated about a hundred years ago, and Mr. Bulleid has now dug into others. His results are not very conclusive, but they seem to imply that the mounds, whatever they were, were not used for pottery making, since among many relics of various sorts no 'wasters' have been found. See further, for an account of the finds in this region, *Victoria Hist. of Somerset*, i. 351-3.

Surrey

(38) The *Surrey Archaelogical Collections* (vol. xxvi) note various small Roman finds—Roman bricks in the walls of Fetcham Church, possibly Roman plaster at Stoke D'Abernon Church (p. 123), some [56] thirty coins and Roman urns and glass from Ewell (pp. 135, 148), and an urn from Camberwell (p. 149). The same journal (vol. xxvii, p. 155) notes the discovery, not hitherto recorded, of over 100 coins of A.D. 296-312 in an urn dug up in 1904 at Normandy Manor Nurseries, near Guildford.

(39) A *Schedule of Antiquities in the County of Surrey*, by Mr. P. M. Johnston (Guildford, 1913), seems intended for students of mediaeval and modern antiquities, and says little about Roman remains; it has no index and cites no authorities.

Sussex

(40) A Roman well has been examined near Ham Farm, between Hassocks railway station and Hurstpierpoint. It was 38 feet deep, the upper part round and lined with local blue clay, the lower part square and lined with stout oak planks. The only object recorded from it is a 'first century vase', taken out at half-way down, which suggests that the well collapsed at an early date. Another well, flint-lined, was noted near but not explored; Roman potsherds were picked up not far off (*Sussex Archaeological Collections*, lvi. 197). The remains probably belong to a farm detected close by in 1857 (*S. A. C.* xiv. 178). Traces of Roman civilized life are comparatively common in this neighbourhood.

(41) Mr. R. G. Roberts' volume, *The Place-names of Sussex* (Cambridge University Press, 1914), much resembles the Derbyshire monograph noted above (No. 7). Its selection of place-names is about as limited and its neglect of all but purely phonetic considerations is as marked. Names such as Cold Waltham (beside a Roman road), Adur, Lavant, Arun, Chanctonbury, Mount Caburn, do not find a place in it. From a full criticism by Dr. H. Bradley in the *English Historical Review* (xxx. 161-6) one would infer that its philology, too, is by no means satisfactory.

Westmorland

(42) The *Transactions of the Cumberland and Westmorland Antiquarian and Archaeological Society* (xiv. 433-65) contain the first Report, by Mr. R. G. Collingwood, of the excavation of the Roman fort at Borrans Ring, near Ambleside, covering the period from August 1913 to April 1914. It is an excellent piece of description and well illustrated; due attention is given to the small objects; the whole is scholarly and satisfactory. It is perhaps as well to add [57] that one or two details first found in April 1914 were further explored in the following August, and some corrections were obtained which will be published in the second Report. For the rest see above, p. 10.

Wilts.

(43) I have contributed to the *Proceedings of the Bath and District Branch of the Somersetshire Archaeological Society and Natural History* for 1914 (p. 50) a note on the relief of Diana found at Nettleton Scrub, to much the same effect as the paragraph on this sculpture in my Report for 1913 (p. 49).

(44) The *Proceedings of the Society of Antiquaries of London* (xxvi. 209) contain a note by Mr. E. H. Binney on Roman remains on the known Roman site, Nythe Farm, about three miles east of Swindon.

Worcestershire

(45) The same *Proceedings* (xxvi. 206) contain an account by Dr. G. B. Grundy of two sections which he dug lately across the line of Rycknield Street on the high ground south-east of Broadway, thereby helping to fix the road at this point. A sketch-map is added.

Yorkshire

(46) In the *Bradford Antiquary* for October 1914 (iv. 117-34) Dr. F. Villy continues his inquiries into a supposed Roman road running past Harden, a little north-west of Bradford. Dr. Villy actually excavates for his roads, in very praiseworthy fashion. But I do not feel sure that he has actually proved a Roman road on the line which he has here examined; he has found interesting and indubitable traces of an old road, but not decisive evidence of its date. The same volume includes a note of eight Roman coins of the 'Thirty Tyrants', from Yew Bank, Utley.

Wales

(47) *Archaeologia Cambrensis* for 1914 (series vi, vol. xiv) contains useful papers on Roman remains. Mr. H. G. Evelyn White describes in detail his excavations carried out at Castell Collen in 1913 – see my Report for that year, pp. 1-58. One must regret that they have not been continued in 1914. Mr. F. N. Pryce describes his work at [58] Cae Gaer, near Llangurig (pp. 205-20), also noted in that Report. The Rev. J. Fisher quotes place-names possibly indicative of a Roman road near St. Asaph, and quotes a suggestion by Mr. Egerton Phillimore that the township name Wigfair, once Wicware, stands for Gwig-wair, and that the second half of this represents the name Varis which the Antonine Itinerary places on the Roman road from

Chester to Carnarvon at a point which cannot be far from St. Asaph and the Clwydd river (see my *Military Aspects of Roman Wales*, pp. 26-8, and Owen's forthcoming *Pembrokeshire*, ii. 524). Lastly, Mr. J. Ward reports on further finds of the fort wall at Cardiff Castle (pp. 407-10): see above, p. 21.

(48) The excavation of the Roman fort at Gellygaer, thirteen miles north of Cardiff, was brought in 1913 to a point at which (as I learn) it is considered to be for the present finished. I referred to it in my Report for 1913; Mr. John Ward's full description of the results obtained in 1913 is now issued in the *Transactions of the Cardiff Naturalists' Society* (vol. xlvi). The principal finds were a supposed 'drillground' on the north-east of the fort, a bit of another inscription of Trajan, a kiln in the churchyard, and a largish earthwork on the north-west of the fort. This last is a regular oblong of not quite five acres internal area, fortified by an earthen mound and a ditch; trenching across the interior showed no trace of buildings or indeed of any occupation, but the search was not carried very far. Several explanations have been offered of it — that it was a temporary affair, thrown up while the actual fort was abuilding; that it was intended for troops marching past and needing to camp for a night at the spot; that it was an earlier fort, begun when the first invasion of the Silures was made, about A.D. 50-2, but never finished. This third view is Mr. Ward's own. Without more excavation, it is rash to pronounce positively, and perhaps even a minute search might be fruitless. Analogies somewhat favour the first theory, but there will always be room for difference of opinion in explaining these excrescences (so to speak) of permanent forts, which are slight in themselves and slightly explored.

As the exploration of this site appears to be closed for the present, and indeed is nearly complete, it may be convenient to give a conspectus of the whole in a small plan (fig. 29).

(49) The fourth volume issued by the Welsh Monuments Commission (*Inventory of Ancient Monuments in the County of Denbigh*, H.M. Stationery Office, 1914) enumerates the few Roman remains of Denbighshire. The one important item is the group of tile and pottery kilns lately excavated by Mr. A. Acton at Holt, eight miles

[59]

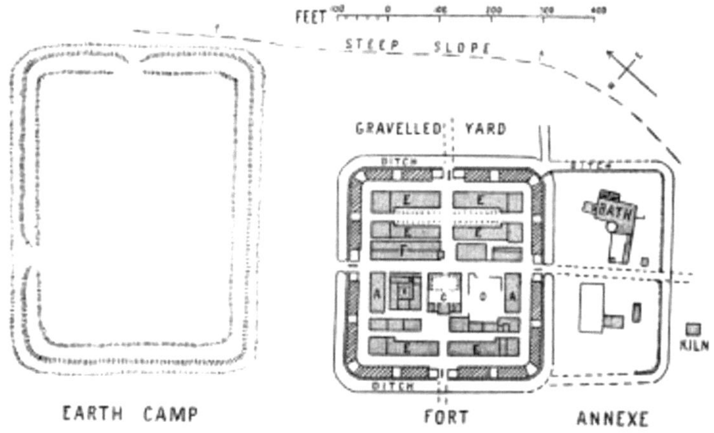

Fig. 29. General Plan of Roman Works at Gellygaer (Glamorgan) (A. Granaries; B. Commandant's House; C. Headquarters; D. doubtful; E. Barracks; F. Stabling(?))

[60]

south of Chester, which I have described above (p. 15); the Commissioners' plan of the site seems to have an incorrect scale. Chance finds, important if not yet fully understood, have been found in British camps at Pen-y-corddin, Moel Fenlli, Moel y Gaer, and especially at Parc-y-Meirch or Dinorben (above, p. 28). Isolated coins have been found scantily—a hoard of perhaps 6,000 Constantinian copper at Moel Fenlli, a gold coin of Nero from the same hill, another coin of Nero at Llanarmon, 200-300 Constantinian at Llanelidan. A parcel of bronze 'cooking vessels' was found near Abergele (Eph. Epigr. iii. 130) but has unfortunately disappeared. The index also mentions coins under 'No. 458', which does not appear in the volume itself. A Roman road probably ran across the county from St. Asaph to Caerhyn (Canovium); its east end is pretty certain, as far as Glascoed, though the 'Inventory' hardly makes this clear.

(50) A partial plan and some views of the west gate of the Roman fort at the Gaer, near Brecon, are given in the *Transactions of the Woolhope Naturalists' Field Club* for 1908-11.

(51) The fifth Report of the Royal Commission on Ancient and Historical Monuments in Scotland, *Inventory of Monuments in Galloway. II. Stewartry of Kirkcudbright* (Edinburgh, 1914) shows that the eastern half of Galloway, like the western half described in the fourth Report in 1912, contains nothing that can be called a 'Roman site' and very few Roman remains of any sort. Indeed this eastern half, the land between Dumfries and Newton Stewart, seems even poorer in such remains than the district between Newton Stewart and the Irish Sea. Its only items are some trifles of Samian, &c., found in the Borness Cave, and some iron implements found in a bronze caldron in Carlingwark Loch. This result is, of course, contrary to the views of older Scottish writers like Skene, who talked of 'numerous Roman camps and stations' in Galloway, but it will surprise no recent student. Probably the Romans never got far west of a line roughly coinciding with that of the Caledonian Railway from Carlisle by Carstairs to Glasgow. Their failure or omission to hold the south-west weakened the left flank and rear of their position on the Wall of Pius and helped materially to shorten their dominion in Scotland in the second century.

(52) In the *Proceedings of the Society of Antiquaries of Scotland* for 1913-4 (vol. xlviii) Mr. J. M. Corrie describes some polishers and [61] other small objects found casually at Newstead (p. 338), and Dr. Macdonald expands (p. 395) the account of the Balcreggan hoard which he had contributed to the *Scotsman* (my Report for 1913, p. 11). Mr. A. O. Curle (p. 161) records the discovery and exploration of a vitrified fort at the Mote of Mark near Dalbeattie (Kirkcudbright), and the discovery in it of two clearly Roman potsherds. The main body of the finds made here seem to belong to the ninth century; whether any of them can be earlier than has been thought, I am not competent to decide.

(53) The well-known and remarkable earthworks at Birrenswark, near Lockerbie in Dumfriesshire, have long been explained as a Roman circumvallation 13 or at least as siege-works round a native hill-fort. In 1913 they were visited by Prof. Schulten, of Erlangen, the excavator of a Roman circumvallation round the Spanish fortress of Numantia; they naturally interested him, and he has now

described them for German readers (*Neue Jahrbücher für das klassische Altertum*, xxxiii, 1914, pp. 607-17) and added some remarks on their date. His description is clear and readable; his chronological arguments are less satisfactory. He adopts 14 the view generally adopted by English archaeologists (except Roy) for the last two centuries, that these camps date from Agricola; he supports this old conclusion by reasons which are in part novel. I may summarize his position thus: Two Roman roads led from the Tyne and the Solway to Caledonia, an eastern road by Corbridge and Newstead, and a western one by Annandale and Upper Clydesdale. On the eastern road, a little north of Newstead, is the camp of Channelkirk; on the western are the three camps of Torwood Moor (near Lockerbie), Tassie's Holm (north of Moffat), and Cleghorn in Clydesdale, near Carstairs. These four camps are — so far as preserved — of the same size, 1,250 × 1,800 feet; they all have six gates (two in each of the longer sides); they all have traverses in front of the gates; lastly, Torwood Moor is fourteen Roman miles, a day's march, from Tassie's Holm, and that is twenty-eight miles from Cleghorn. Plainly they belong to the same date. Further, Agricola is the only Roman general who used both eastern and western routes together; accordingly, these camps date from him. Finally, as Birrenswark is near Torwood Moor, it too must be Agricolan.

[62]

Dr. Schulten has not advanced matters by this speculation. His first point, that the four camps are coeval, and his reasons for that idea, are mainly taken from Roy — he does not make this clear in his paper. But he has not heeded Roy's warnings that the reasons are not cogent. Actually, they are very weak. At Channelkirk, only two sides of a camp remained in Roy's time; they measured not 1,250 × 1,800 feet but 1,330 × 1,660 feet, and the longer side had one gate in the middle, not two; to-day, next to nothing is visible. At Tassie's Holm there was only a corner of a perhaps quite small earthwork — not necessarily Roman — and the distance to Torwood Moor is nearer twenty than fourteen Roman miles. At Torwood Moor only one side, 1,780 feet long with two gates, was clear in Roy's time; the width of the camp is unknown. Cleghorn seems to have been fairly complete, but modern measurers give its size as 1,000 × 1,700 feet. Dr. Schulten builds on imaginary foundations when he calls these four camps coeval. He has not even proof that there were four camps.

Nor is his reason any more convincing for assigning these camps, and Birrenswark with them, to Agricola. Here he parts company from Roy and adduces an argument of his own—that Agricola was the only general who used both eastern and western routes. That is a mere assertion, unproven and improbable. Roman generals were operating in Scotland in the reigns of Pius and Marcus (A.D. 140-80) and Septimius Severus; if there were two routes, it is merely arbitrary to limit these men to the eastern route. As a matter of fact, the history of the western route is rather obscure; doubts have been thrown on its very existence north of Birrens. But if it did exist, the sites most obviously connected with it are the second-century sites of Birrens, Lyne, and Carstairs; at Birrenswark itself the only definitely datable finds, four coins, include two issues of Trajan. 15

The truth is that the question is more complex than Dr. Schulten has realized. Possibly it is not ripe for solution. I have myself ventured, in previous publications, to date Birrenswark to Agricola— for reasons quite different from those of Dr. Schulten. But I would emphasize that we need, both there and at many earth-camps, full [63] archaeological use of the spade. The circumstances of the hour are unfavourable to that altogether.

Postscript

Herefordshire

(54) As I go to press, I receive the *Transactions of the Woolhope Naturalists' Field Club* for 1908-11 (Hereford, 1914), a volume which, despite the date on its title-page, does not appear to have been actually issued till April 1915. It contains on pp. 68-73 and 105-9 two illustrated papers on three Roman roads of Herefordshire—Stone Street, the puzzling road near Leominster, and Blackwardine, the itinerary route between Gloucester and Monmouth. The find made at Donnington in 1906, which is explained on p. 69 as a 'villa' and on p. 109 as an agrimensorial pit—this latter an impossibility—was, I think, really a kiln, though there may have been a dwelling-house near. The most interesting of the Roman finds made lately in Herefordshire, those of Kenchester, do not come into this volume, but belong in point of date to the volume which will succeed it.

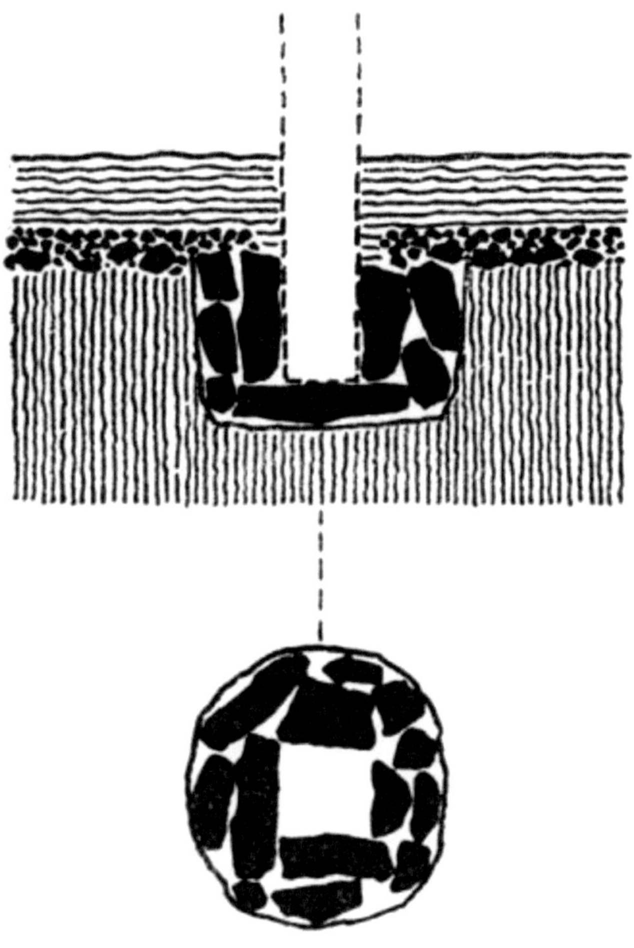

Fig. 30. Gellygaer. Stone Packing for a Wooden Posthole in the Verandah of the Barracks (Fig. 29 e)

[64]

APPENDIX: LIST OF PERIODICALS

The following list enumerates the archaeological and other periodicals published in these islands which sometimes or often contain noteworthy articles relating to Roman Britain. Those which contained such articles in 1914 are marked by an asterisk, and references are given in square brackets to the numbered paragraphs in the preceding section (pp. 38-63).

1. Periodicals not connected with special districts

Archaeologia (Society of Antiquaries of London).

**Proceedings of the Society of Antiquaries of London* [see 30, 37, 44, 45].

English Historical Review (London).

Scottish Historical Review (Glasgow).

**Numismatic Chronicle* (London) [see 8].

British Numismatic Journal (London).

**Journal of Roman Studies* (London) [see 28].

**Archaeological Journal* (Royal Archaeological Institute, London) [see 2].

**Journal of the British Archaeological Association* (London) [see 17, 24, 30].

**Antiquary* (London) [see 3, 32].

Athenaeum (London).

Architectural Review (London).

2. Periodicals dealing primarily with special districts

Berkshire. *Berks, Bucks, and Oxon Archaeological Journal* (Reading) [see 5].

Buckinghamshire. *Records of Buckinghamshire* (Aylesbury). See also Berks.

Cambridgeshire. *Proceedings of the Cambridge Antiquarian Society* (Cambridge).

Proceedings of the Cambridge and Huntingdonshire Archaeological Society (Ely).

Cheshire. *Journal of the Architectural, Archaeological, and Historic Society of Chester and North Wales* (Chester).

See also Lancashire.

Cornwall. *Journal of the Royal Institution of Cornwall* (Plymouth). See also Devon.

Cumberland. *Transactions of the Cumberland and Westmorland Antiquarian and Archaeological Society* (Kendal). Includes also Lancashire north of the Sands [see 42].

Derbyshire. *Journal of the Derbyshire Archaeological and Natural History Society* (Derby) [see 7].

Devon. *Report and Transactions of the Devon Association* (Plymouth).

Devon and Cornwall Notes and Queries (Exeter).

Dorset. *Proceedings of the Dorset Natural History and Antiquarian Field Club* (Dorchester) [see 8, 9].

[65]

Durham. *Proceedings of the University of Durham Philosophical Society* (Newcastle-on-Tyne).

See also Northumberland, *Archaeologia Aeliana*.

Essex. *Transactions of the Essex Archaeological Society* (Colchester) [see 10, 11].

Essex Review (Colchester).

Proceedings of the Prehistoric Society of East Anglia (London).

Gloucestershire. *Transactions of the British and Gloucestershire Archaeological Society* (Bristol) [see 12].

Hampshire. *Proceedings of the Hampshire Field Club and Archaeological Society* (Southampton) [see 14, 15].

Herefordshire. *Transactions of the Woolhope Naturalists' Field Club* (Hereford) [see 50, 54].

Hertford. *Transactions of the East Herts Archaeological Society* (Hertford) [see 16].

Huntingdonshire. See under Cambridgeshire.

Kent. *Archaeologia Cantiana*, Transactions of the Kent Archaeological Society (London) [see 17].

Transactions of the Greenwich Antiquarian Society (London) [see 18].

Lancashire. *Transactions of the Lancashire and Cheshire Antiquarian Society* (Manchester) [see 19, 20].

Transactions of the Lancashire and Cheshire Historic Society (Liverpool).

(For Lancashire north of the Sands see also Cumberland.)

Leicestershire. *Transactions of the Leicestershire Archaeological Society* (Leicester).

Reports and Papers of the Architectural Societies of Lincoln, York, Northampton and Oakham, Worcester and Leicester, called Associated Architectural Societies (Lincoln).

Lincolnshire. *Lincolnshire Notes and Queries* (Horncastle) [see 21, 22].

See also under Leicestershire.

London and Middlesex. *Transactions of the London and Middlesex Archaeological Society* (London).

London Topographical Record (London).

Norfolk. *Norfolk Archaeology* (Norfolk and Norwich Archaeological Society, Norwich).

See also under Essex.

Northants. *Northamptonshire Notes and Queries* (London).

See also under Leicestershire.

Northumberland. *Archaeologia Aeliana* (Society of Antiquaries of Newcastle-on-Tyne, Newcastle) [see 30].

Proceedings of the same Society.

Notts. *Transactions of the Thornton Society* (Nottingham).

Oxfordshire. *Oxford Archaeological Society* (Banbury).

See also under Berkshire.

Rutland. See under Leicestershire.

Shropshire. *Transactions of the Shropshire Archaeological and Natural History Society* (Shrewsbury).

Somerset. *Proceedings of the Somersetshire Archaeological and Natural History Society* (Taunton) [see 35].

[66]

Proceedings of the Bath and District Branch, of the Somersetshire Archaeological Society (Bath) [see 43].

Notes and Queries for Somerset and Dorset (Sherborne) [see 36].

Staffordshire. *Annual Report and Transactions of the North Staffordshire Field Club* (Stafford).

Suffolk. *Proceedings of the Suffolk Institute of Archaeology and Natural History* (Ipswich).

See also under Essex.

Surrey. *Surrey Archaeological Collections* (London) [see 38].

Sussex. *Sussex Archaeological Collections* (Brighton) [see 39].

Warwickshire. *Transactions of the Birmingham and Midland Institute* (Birmingham).

Westmorland. See under Cumberland.

Wiltshire. *Wiltshire Archaeological and Natural History Magazine* (Devizes).

Wiltshire Notes and Queries (Devizes).

Worcestershire. See under Leicestershire.

Yorkshire. *Yorkshire Archaeological Journal* (Yorkshire Archaeological Society, Leeds).

Publications of the Thoresby Society (Leeds).

**The Bradford Antiquary* (Bradford) [see 46].

Transactions of the Hunter Archaeological Society (Sheffield).

Wales. **Archaeologia Cambrensis* (Cambrian Archaeological Association, London) [see 47].

Montgomeryshire Collections (Oswestry).

Transactions of the Honourable Society of Cymmrodorion and *Y-Cymmrodor* (London).

Carmarthenshire Antiquarian Society and Field Club Transactions (Carmarthen).

**Report and Transactions of the Cardiff Naturalists' Society* (Cardiff) [see 48].

Scotland. **Proceedings of the Society of Antiquaries of Scotland* (Edinburgh) [see 52].

Transactions of the Glasgow Archaeological Society (Glasgow).

**Proceedings of the Berwickshire Naturalists' Field Club* (Alnwick) [see 31].

[67]

Footnotes

<u>1</u> (return)

Antiquities, plate 50. Roy does not notice it in his text, any more than he notices plate 51 (Ythan Wells camp). They are the two last plates in his volume; as this was issued posthumously in 1793 (he died in 1790), perhaps the omission is intelligible.

<u>2</u> (return)

I saw this verandah while open. The whole excavations at Caersws yielded important results and it is more than regrettable that no report of them has ever been issued.

<u>3</u> (return)

A Bronze Age burial (fig. 6, D) suggests that the clay may have been worked long before the Romans.

<u>4</u> (return)

References are given by Watkin, *Cheshire*, p. 305, and Palmer, *Archaeologia Cambrensis*, 1906, pp. 225 foll.

<u>5</u> (return)

The words Church, Chapel, and Chantry often form parts of the names of Roman sites, where the ruined masonry has been popularly mistaken for that of deserted ecclesiastical buildings.

<u>6</u> (return)

I may refer to my *Romanization of Britain* (third edition, p. 77). This does not, of course, mean that they were not also occupied earlier.

<u>7</u> (return)

It has been styled the 'basilical' type, but few names could be less suitable.

<u>8</u> (return)

As to Bainbridge see my paper in the *Cumberland and Westmorland Archaeological Transactions*, new series, vol. xi (1911), pp. 343-78.

<u>9</u> (return)

See an excellent paper by Cumont, *Revue d'Histoire et de Littérature religieuses*, 1896, pp. 435-52.

<u>10</u> (return)

Sir Laurence alludes (p. 77) to a Caerwent inscription as unpublished. It has probably appeared in print a dozen times; I have had the misfortune to publish it three times over myself. Its meaning is not quite correctly stated on p. 77.

11 (return)
Compare the Roman provincial bas-reliefs of Actaeon surprising
Diana, with Actaeon omitted (R. Cagnat, *Archaeological Journal*, lxiv.
42).
12 (return)
By the courtesy of the publisher of the *Antiquary*, Mr. Elliot Stock, I
am able to reproduce two of these illustrations (figs. 23, 24).
13 (return)
It is proper to add a warning that the traces of the 'circumvallation'
are dim, and high authorities like Dr. Macdonald are sceptical about
them. The two camps are, however, certain, and there must have
been communication between them of some sort, if they were occupied at the same time.
14 (return)
No doubt it is by oversight that Dr. Schulten omits to state that the
view which he is supporting is the ordinary view and not his own.
15 (return)
Gordon, p. 184, *Minutes of the Soc. Antiq.* i. 183 (2 February, 1725). It
has been suggested that Gordon mixed up Birrens and Birrenswark.
But though the Soc. Antiq. Minutes only describe the coins as 'found
in a Roman camp in Annandale, ... the first Roman camp to be seen
in Scotland', Gordon obviously knew more than the Minutes contain—he gives, e.g. the name of a local antiquary who noted the
find—and the distinction between the 'town' (as it was then
thought) of Middelby (as it was then called) and the camp of
Burnswork, was well recognized in his time.